The
Ultimate Game
of Golf

How to Master Golf's Outer,
Inner and Scoring Games

The
Ultimate Game
of Golf

How to Master Golf's Outer,
Inner and Scoring Games

By Bob Cisco

FIRST EDITION

Griffin Publishing
Glendale, California

10 9 8 7 6 5 4

Grateful acknowledgment is made to L. Ron Hubbard Library for permission to reproduce sections from the copyrighted works of L. Ron Hubbard. *Dianetics, Scientology, Hubbard* an *OT* are trademarks and service marks owned by RTC and are used with its permission.

ISBN 1-882180-38-0
Library of Congress No. 92-083746
Cisco, Robert F.
Editor: Andre Makovsky
Illustrator: Anne Fewell
Cover Design: Jan Guildersleeve
Book Design & Electronic Production : MasterDesign Los Angeles
Photo Credits: Bill Hardman
Cover Photograph: Tony Roberts
Cover Photo courtesy of Sugerloaf Country Club, Maine
Illustrations on pages 14, 37 & 45 were based on drawings from the book
How to Perfect Your Golf Swing by Jim Ballard
Manufactured in the United States of America

Dedication

This book is dedicated to my dad,
who taught me how to play the game
and reminded me golf is a game;
my mom for her support and patience;
and to my daughter Crystal,
for her being there through it all.

Contents

SECTION III: THE STATEGY SCORING GAME

Acknowledgements

Writing a book is usually a one-person task, but producing it requires a sharing of talents by several people. Such was the case with this book, and there are certain people I particularly want to thank.

As a writer and student of the mind I owe a special note of gratitude to L. Ron Hubbard for his indispensable technology of the mind. In the years since I first read his best selling work *Dianetics: The Modern Science of Mental Health,* I have experienced improvement in my outlook and abilities both personally and professionally.

The philosophy of winning contained in this book is the result of intensive study and observation of what works in mental performance and is to a large degree derived from this technology.

I want to thank André Makovsky. Not only do I value his expertise as an editor—more importantly—his encouragement and support were always there for me as the writer.

I am very grateful to Anne Fewell for her meticulous attention to detail in creating the numerous illustrations that were integral to this book; also her patience in getting all the swing photos just right.

Grateful acknowledgement is given to golf professional, Mike D. Dingwell for providing the many swing poses and shots from which the artist was able to draw from.

I would also like to acknowledge the following two individuals who assisted me learn and get around on my personal computer during my early days with the Word Star word processing program and later on when my "pc decided to go on its own vacation." These are Steven Huelsman and Bill Hardman.

In addition to the above individuals, I want to thank Jan Gildersleeve for her cover design, which was outstanding.

The drills and exercises contained herewithin are intended as tools for improving your game. They are offered for your use with the hope that you, too, will achieve enjoyment and ability in this great game that is golf.   —Bob Cisco

Credits

I thank the following authors and publishers for permission to use quotes from their publications, which enriched this present work: Dr. Gideon Ariel, *The Biomechanics of Power Golf;* Jim Ballard, *How To Perfect Your Golf Swing,* Golf Digest Books; Percy Boomer, *On Learning Golf,* Random House Books; Frank W. Jobe, M.D. and Diane R. Moynes, M.S., R.P.T., *30 Exercises for Better Golf,* Champion Press; Robert T. Jones, *Golf is My Game,* Doubleday Books; David Leadbetter, *The Golf Swing,* Viking Penguin/USA, Inc.; Jack Nicklaus, *Golf My Way,* Golden Bear Publishing.

Thanks is also given to Jim Ballard for several illustrations used in Section I from his work, *How To Perfect Your Golf Swing.*

Special thanks is given to Bridge Publications for permission to quote from the works of L. Ron Hubbard, especially from, *Dianetics: The Modern Science of Mental Health.*

Foreword

As an athlete I have been playing professional golf for the past five years on the Golden State and Spalding Tours in California. From my experience I can say that there is no other sport or contest that requires you to rise to such physical and mental excellence. Golf is very much the ultimate of all games.

In order to be my best as a touring pro, I have read many a book on golf and have sought out the finest in instruction. This brings me to Bob Cisco. I first met Bob in 1988 at which time he helped me with my mental approach. After a few sessions that year, I started winning on Tour and had some of my best finishes. In my opinion, I haven't met anyone who understood the game of golf better and knew more about how to play to win than Bob.

Since then, I have come to recognize what it takes to win and have done so, winning more than ten tournaments. This has been most evident in my mental game, in which Bob has given me the feeling of power, control and the all important feeling of certainty.

In addition to this, Bob helped transform my putting from being a good putter to a super one based on feel and in doing so I felt a renewed sense of confidence in sinking putts. I started holing more chips as well. Along with this, I experience improvement in my wedge shot from under 100 yards, which I can now stick close to the pin with authority to cash in on more birdies.

Bob has a gift as a teacher, adviser and writer to communicate golf in a powerful but simple way. There is no question in my mind that simplicity enhances performance. Bob understands this and has taught me to approach difficulty situations in my golf with a calmness and clarity of mind. This has really strengthened my game and has helped me be more decisive in my shot-making. This truly is the winning approach I've been looking for. This powerful feeling can be tapped for all golfers to experience in their games.

Golf is a game of sportsmanship and integrity. This is something that Bob has instilled in me, to play the game from a spirit of play. I've been playing the game for many years now and I can honestly now say there's a state of mind that's needed to play your best and this is something that Bob communicates so well in his new book, *The Ultimate Game of Golf.*

For the past several years, Bob Cisco has had excellent results as an instructor and advisor to top amateurs and pros on Tour. His players have won over twenty tournaments and have had over sixty-five top ten finishes using his methods.

Besides his ability to teach, Bob has a special quality to bring the best out of each of his players and in producing winning performances. I highly recommend this book!

Thanks for everything,

> Jeff Anderson,
> 1992 Southern California Open Champion

The Ultimate Game of Golf

Introduction

I had been thinking of quitting the game. Actually, I had been thinking this way for some time. Nothing seemed to work, not even the golf lessons and the new clubs I had bought. My game was suffering and was stuck in a rut. Yet there was a part of me that knew I could play this game, and said to not give up.

Something had to change and I needed it to happen soon or else. Perhaps I should give up golf for something less painful, something that would give back some enjoyment for all my toil. If only there was a break-through for me towards a more consistent game instead of this anguish. I needed a weapon, a new game.

And then it happened. It was incredible. Unlike anything I had ever experienced...something so out of my normal way of playing golf that I'll never forget it. I doubt if I will ever be quite the same again.

There I was making the turn after nine and proceeding out on the back nine, approaching another tee, this one the 13th, a long dogleg left, coming off three consecutive birdies and an eagle that I had made at the par five eight where I got home in two for the first time and holed the putt. There was a lone par I might add in between this string of sub-par holes.

I just couldn't believe it—the long drive, the three wood coming to rest within seven feet of the cup, followed by the eagle putt right in back of the hole as if it had eyes. Everything felt oh so right. A calmness and clarity, a oneness of mind and spirit seemed to grace my every move.

An ecstatic joy raced through my soul, adrenalin flowing like never before. Five under in a span of five holes! Having not only closed out our

1

stunned opponents for the nine, I figured that I was three under on my own ball, my lowest score for nine holes! I could have been five under if it hadn't been for the penalty stroke at the fourth hole and the missed four foot putt for par the hole before.

I quickly came to the realization that this was my first sub-par round of golf and assault against "Old Man Par." Yet nine tough holes remained and a lot can go wrong in golf especially with what laid in store on the final closing holes, a voice of experience suddenly beckoned to me.

An unbelievable feeling of power and confidence continued to surge through me as I knew I was about to unleash yet another drive down the fairway. A sense of power so effortless, yet so simple and direct was present; I was in a zone, a state of mind directly tied to action, my awareness heightened and my ability to concentrate was superb.

The sensitivity of my hands and clubs was beyond description, a marriage of mind and feel, a knowingness that I was about to unleash another big drive, and make another putt, each stroke another opportunity to score... I was thinking not just for par but the opportunity to birdie. I felt invincible. It was unreal, what an experience. I had my best score at 69, three under par for the day! My first conquering of "Old Man Par"! How great life can be. Golf is the greatest of human pursuits!

Time had taken on a new dimension. The light in the forward room of the clubhouse dimmed more as the shadow grew longer on the wall opposite me, yet the light was momentarily harsh to my eyes as I sought to refocus. The proportions of the room started to now return to their normal dimensions in size and shape.

A voice close to the chair light and soothing to my ear, nearly a whisper now as if not to disturb me from my reverie, said to me, "What you have experienced my golfing friend in your most recent round of golf is a *close encounter of the golf kind.*"

This is an experience that you like other golfers, have had where you have played out or played part of a round of golf, in which something extraordinary happened, encountering a state of mind that is out of your normal state of being or operation, a state of mind of heightened awareness, sensitivity of touch and an acute ability to focus, concentrate and play golf far above your normal level.

This state of mind is usually accompanied by a flurry of emotions—

emotional tones such as exhilaration, intense interest and action, serenity and a "spirit of play," something not usually part of the seriousness of the human condition so caught up in the efforts of life's existence.

This mental state is a subjective state of mind and its occurrences are relative in degree with each golfer's experience, and are subject to a set of natural laws that govern the performance of the mind itself.

In 1994, over 9,864,392: (an approximate figure found by the author in which golfers experienced "a close encounter of the golf kind.") incidents were reported by golfers like yourself of experiences, similar in some respect to what happened to the golfer above; the figures are most likely higher in actuality.

A close encounter of the golf kind is an incident, an experience in which the golfer has encountered either 1) a stellar golf shot that came off as planned; 2) a consecutive run of pars or birdie; or 3) an eagle, double eagle, or hole in one in golf.

These incidents were in most cases witnessed by another in one's playing group or by a bystander—these were real incidents experienced by such golfers. These golfers were never quite the same afterwards...the experience changed their lives in more than one way. In each case the person reported being in an extraordinary state of mind and in a "zone" far removed from the mainstream of experience.

Over the years I've compiled a number of accounts and reports from golfers of all levels on the mental approach to golf. I became intrigued with this part of the game and convinced that it is something that can be harnessed and tapped. Such close encounters of the golf kind would be a series of down-to-earth encounters of regular occurrences that the golfer could produce. Armed with the true knowledge of the swing and the mental approach, the golfer can apply the power of the information that is described in this book to his game and have an "Ultimate Game of Golf" at their disposal.

I do think golfers can arrive at a closer union with such a power of the mind that will help them think more clearly, and manage their fears, upsetting memories, and any sense of failure that they have in their game. Essentially, it will make them more self-confident, and more in control of their golf games and lives.

Golf is a game of many diverse shots and situations that require a keen sense of intellect and savvy to excel at. There is an "instinct" that good players develop that brings their necessity level to its peak that is the ultimate challenge to the player who makes the shot happen.

Golf is a game that many feel is the most challenging and difficult of all sports to master. It may well be the ultimate of all games for the individual sportsman, requiring him to draw upon all his skills and resourcefulness in order to excel. All good players of the game from the great legendary players to the good amateur golfer, recognize the importance of the mental approach to golf.

Why this book?

The purpose of this book lies in the age old question in this game of golf that you have most often asked yourself and others that why amongst golfers with equal ability, some were winners and others were losers—why even some players with lesser physical abilities were still winners. What did these players know, use, and how were they able to accomplish more than the rest of us?

Is there a way to reach more of our potential, play smarter and learn more enjoyable golf, to have a significant competitive edge, to have the "Ultimate Game of Golf" in one's game?

The answer is Yes! There is a better way, and you can win at your golf and be successful.

You can play better, smarter and more enjoyable golf and not only astonish your golfing friends but play far beyond your current level and achieve goals in your game that you only dreamed were possible.

"The Ultimate Game of Golf" Golfer is one who is armed and dangerous to one's opponents, who has the knowledge and control of an efficient swing, has the right mental attitude on the course, can think smart under pressure, and be decisive in strategy and shot-making.

There are three major sections of *The Ultimate Game of Golf* book. Each part is designed with the utmost information to rocket you to the success you know you are truly capable of reaching in your game.

Part I is The Outer Game, the swing and its fundamentals; Part II The Inner Game, the mental approach; and Part III is The Scoring, (strategy) Game.

How To Use This Book

The Ultimate Game of Golf book covers a broad spectrum of the game of golf. The game of golf is categorized into three major parts. These are the Outer Game of Golf, The Inner Game/Mental Approach, and The Strategy/Scoring Game.

Each section has an outline which highlights the material for the golfer to follow and should be done in the order that it appears as you progress through the text. The drills as a rule should be done individually before going to the next and any uncertainties handled before progressing to the next section.

The first section of the book contains the Swing Fundamentals and Natural Laws of Movement for successful study of the swing along with its accompanied drills. Each drill is designed to work on a specific area of the swing and in building a strong understanding of its mechanics. Drills have a specific purpose[1] in mind, an emphasis[2] (training stress), and end result.[3]

In order to have the "Ultimate Game of Golf," you the golfer have to fully master each section starting with the swing fundamentals as outlined in this section. A solid foundation is needed in the swing before you can progress to the next level Section II, the Inner Game/Mental Approach.

The golfer will find that the number of times through each section and its parts will elicit newer awarenesses, realizations of the game and mastery of it. They are to be studied and drilled over and over from the beginning in building "Your Ultimate Game of Golf."

Section II contains the theory and drills that comprise the Mental Approach that is needed to play your best. Follow the outline in this section in the sequence that is laid out.

Section III the Scoring Game comprises the third and final section of the book. It covers effective course management and strategy. You'll learn to

1. purpose; aim; intention
2. emphasis: stress; importance
3. end result: outcome or result

think smarter and become a scoring threat in your game. Use the theory and drills here to sharpen these skills for better scores in your game.

At the end of the book you will find a Player's Profile section that highlights successes from a cross section of players who have used *The Ultimate Game of Golf* book to their benefit. Each profile highlights a specific part or principle from the program that worked successfully for them in their game.

There is a Glossary in the back of the book for reference that defines words as used in the book.

Lastly, there is a section entitled, About the Book and the Author. This closing section entails how the book was conceived, compiled, and brought together in final form, and some biographical information about the author.

Important Note

In studying *The Ultimate Game of Golf*, be very, very certain you never go past a word you do not understand. If the material becomes confusing or you can't seem to grasp it, there will be a word just earlier that you have not understood. Don't go any further, but go back to BEFORE you got into trouble, find the misunderstood word and get it defined.

It is also important that you do one step at a time on the drills and that you stick to the sequence that's laid out for you to follow. If you skip ahead you will hit a point where you'll find that you can't apply the next part and you will find yourself confused, unable to go on in your progress.

Wishing you Success in your Golf,
The Editors

Section I

The Outer Game of Golf

SECTION I
THE OUTER GAME OF GOLF

Chapter I

On Learning To Play Better Golf

The purpose of The Outer Game section of *The Ultimate Game of Golf* book is to provide you with the knowledge and understanding of the golf swing, and its fundamentals in harnessing the most effective and powerful swing.

Despite technological advances over the years in golf club and ball design that help the golfer in hitting the ball longer and straighter, it's a fact that golfers have not, as a whole made significant improvement in scoring with all the "hi-tech" advances that are available.

Although I have worked chiefly with the more advanced golfer and his mental approach in more recent years, I've worked with golfers at all levels as an instructor. I compiled a set of statistics over the years that were rather interesting. The one statistic in studying performances that was most significant was the fact that only five percent of these players shoot below 80, and the majority of them, ninety-five percent, don't and will never break or come close to par in their golfing lives! Every golfer is striving to play his best at whatever level he is. Here's a more complete breakdown of this revealing statistic.

Percentage of Golfer's Scores		
Score	Handicap	Percentage
70 – 79	-2 to 7	5%
80 – 89	8 to 17	20%
90 – 99	18 to 27	35%
100 – 129	28 to 37	40%

Although golf as the pros have mastered it is at a level that is difficult to attain for the majority of golfers, the game of golf is more popular today than ever throughout the world. Golf continues to boom, and as the love affair for the game increases golfers can't seem to wait for the sun to come up and head for the links to meet "Old Man Par's" challenge and intrigue!

One of the chief purposes of this book is to discover why golfers as a whole find the game difficult to master and what can be done to assist them in playing to more of their potential.

The great legendary golfers of the game from the golden era of golf from the 1920s–1930s: Jones, Hagen, Sarazen, to name a few, accomplished incredible performances, scoring in the 60s and low 70s using "inferior equipment" compared to what is available today to golfers. Byron Nelson in 1945, about the time in which golf equipment was undergoing some significant changes, won fourteen tournaments that year, and holds the lowest scoring record to date on the PGA Tour of 68.25!

These great players were more than superb ball strikers of the game, they were true professionals, not just great athletes, but artisans who were fine-tuned to their craft. It was not uncommon for these players to spend many an hour reworking their clubs, working on adding weight to their driver, building up a putter grip, grinding the sole of their irons, changing the bounce on their wedge—all in an effort to get the feel just right with their clubs.

These players possessed a high degree of sensitivity and despite playing on many courses that were far from modern standards with watered fairways, they played from an inner sense of purpose and an affinity with their tools of the trade.

It would be rather convenient to actually stop here and state that the problem in golf (in not being able to break eighty for 95% of the golfing populace) has to do with the equipment and its inadequacies, but that isn't true. Golf clubs today are easier and more forgiving to hit; plus ball aerodynamics have improved. The scores that good players of the game were able to muster over the last seventy years in golf with more inferior equipment disproves this premise. So the problem as I have approached it has to do with the actual learning of golf and its instruction.

The game of golf actually consists of three major parts: the Outer Game, the Inner Game and the Scoring Game. The golf swing is the foundation upon which the other two games are played. Each game is interdependent, and functions with the other two for success. To be a good player one needs to master all three games in order to reach one's true potential as a golfer. In studying the many theories and principles of the swing and its mechanics, I found a *missing link* or ingredient having to do with a key principle, without which the golfer has a faulty foundation and will not learn the golf swing to its fullest. This missing link is the reason why golfers are not getting the most out of their games.

There are natural laws in golf (the interaction and formulations of observed phenomena, order, and its recurrences), that need to be fully understood and applied by the golfer in producing consistent, well executed golf shots. It is necessary for the golfer to thoroughly know these key components, and how they interrelate in bringing about "The Ultimate Game of Golf" Swing.

There is a natural law in golf and all sports that involves the throwing or hitting of a ball or object to a target. This law involves the dynamics of movement of the body and the motion of the swinging club.

Each of these sports involves the moving or the swinging of the club in a prescribed manner, maintaining optimum balance and creating a powerful hitting motion that releases the built-up force at the ball at impact and out towards the target.

The movement is essentially the same and follows the principle of moving a club or bat back and through in a balanced manner from the center of the body, and using a hinging mechanism of the arms and wrists, to create a powerful release of motion and clubhead speed into the ball. Centrifugal force[4] plays an integral role in the golf swing in the release of the club as it is returned back to the ball at impact.

We therefore have a law about this:

ANY ATHLETIC MOTION INVOLVING THE SWINGING OF A CLUB CONSISTS OF PLANTING, PIVOTING, AND DRIVING THE BODY IN A BALANCED POSITION INTO THE BALL. MOTION DIRECTED FROM THE CENTER OF THE BODY CREATES OPTIMUM LEVERAGE, CONTROL AND CLUBHEAD SPEED.

4. centrifugal force: the tendency of the swinging golf club to pull away from the center of the body in the forward swing to the target.

The dynamic movement in sports

Thus there are three key motions in the golf swing: Planting, Pivoting, and Driving. Planting is the action of the body setting up firmly in optimum position to strike the ball. It also is the action of setting the left foot down firmly in the forward swing (if you lift the foot up initially in the backswing). Pivoting is the action of turning the torso around the spine in the golf swing. This creates coil. Driving is the action of striking quickly.

Therefore we have a triangle that represents this relationship. Power is the kinetic force generated in the golf swing by the action of Planting, Pivoting, and Driving. Planting + Pivoting + Driving = Power. Each of these is interdependent and affects the other. Power in the golf swing is directly proportional to the degree that these elements are maximized.

The Power Triangle in Golf

P + P + D = Power

In sports such as tennis, baseball, and racquetball the ball acts as the stimulus and focal point in motion for the players to advance or return the ball.

Golf presents a peculiar problem in that the golfer is faced with having to start the swing from a static or still position each time. This is harder to do and requires more skill and application. This is a concern for the higher handicap player, who most often stays too long over the ball trying to figure out how to make the swing, instead of creating a feel and a routine as the better player does to get the swing in motion. Too much thinking over the ball invites a mental freeze and forces a more rigid swing, instead of a fluid motion to the target.

The parts of the golf swing flow together. There is no end of one activity and beginning of another. The swing is a continuous motion, a harmonious flow from start to finish; in other words it is a one-piece action or chain of events.

The good player swings from his body's center of gravity and achieves optimum balance. Recent research involving hi-tech computers confirms this. In his recent book, *The Biomechanics of Power Golf*,[5] this was found to be

The essential actions in the golf swing.

the case... "computer analysis of good players reveals the takeaway[6]...the center of gravity moves first with the swing when under the control of the major muscles."

Furthermore, "The computer reveals that the heavy parts in the lower body, knees, thighs, and hips—start to move towards the ball while the

Powerful drive of the lower body position

5. *The Biomechanics of Power Golf:* A book on the biomechanics of golf, written by Dr. Gideon Ariel
6. takeaway: the backswing, especially its beginning

17

upper body is still rotating and the wrists are still hinging. This creates coil. The lower body which was reactive[7] in the backswing becomes active and initiates the downswing while the upper body is still pivoting and hinging."

7. reactive: tending to be responsive.

Chapter II

Golf's Breakthrough— The Interplay of Held Positions

There's a natural law in golf governing the mechanics of the swing that has to do with the harnessing of power. The concept of power in the golf swing has always been something of interest to me as a player of the game and also as an instructor.

Hitting the ball long and straight captures every golfer's interest, no question. What golfer wouldn't want such a priceless gift.... Hitting the ball long with power and control was something I did not fully understand as a player...until later in my teaching days as an instructor.

Power in the Golf Swing

In my research, I found that power in the golf swing amazingly enough had not been defined and correctly stated. Good players knew

Power in the golf swing and its interplay of held positions

what it felt like to hit a powerful shot and how the swing must be made to produce it, yet power had not been defined over the years in technical know how. After being at wits end for some months over this and amazed at the lack of a definition of it in the golf swing, I recently worked out a basic definition for it that made practical sense.

Here's what I discovered that power in the golf swing is:

> POWER IN THE GOLF SWING
> IS DETERMINED BY THE INTERPLAY OF HELD POSITIONS.
>
> A powerful golf swing is the result of opposing motions and alternating held positions, creating resistance around a fixed center in which a driving motion unleashes force at impact in the golf shot.

The Importance of Interplay, Drive and Held Positions

It is important to fully grasp this principle of the interplay of held positions in order to achieve power in your golf swing and have an "Ultimate Game of Golf" Swing working for you. The key concepts in understanding this are Interplay, Drive, and Held Positions. Let's examine each of these here.

The word Interplay, according to my dictionary means, to interact, to act or react on each other. Drive means to force, thrust into hard and rapidly. Held means maintained in a certain position or relationship. Let's assemble each of these to get the full meaning understood.

Interplay is the all encompassing word because it denotes an on-going continuous action in the harnessing of power in the golf swing. Held refers to the position that the upper and lower body must maintain via the body's center of gravity. This is "the hooked up feeling" or the sensation of connection between the two areas that creates a well timed golf shot.

Think of the interplay this way. The interplay is the active motion of the windup and unloading through the ball, and the held positions are those balance points in the body positions that support, maintain, and keep connected the swing in the movement back and through in hitting the shot—without which the golfer can't synchronize the arm swing and the rotation of the torso (center) in correct coordination.

This comes about in a continuous chain of motion in which the club is swung around the fixed axis point of the spine which creates a buildup of potential energy in the backswing and is then transformed into a powerful thrusting action in the forward swing in which the clubhead is driven into the ball to the target.

Power is proportional to the amount of thrust or drive....

Just as one pedals a bicycle by the amount of effort required in getting the legs to push or drive downward in a continuous manner to turn the wheel, likewise the degree of power in golf is proportional to the amount of thrust or drive that the golfer can generate with the lower body platform (hips, thighs, feet) and to the degree that the left side position can resist this driving and release of the wrists and hands at impact. When this is packaged correctly, centrifugal force can be fully utilized and provides a boost of power in releasing the clubhead into the ball at impact.

The whole trick to the swing is this interaction of held positions in which the golfer creates clubhead speed by driving up against something—that something is the left side position of the body. This is only accomplished however from being in a leveraged position, which is the result of being balanced and moving the positions of the swing from the center of the body.

The upper and lower body positions interact—on the backswing the upper body is an active component whereas the lower position is more passive, on the forward swing the roles reverse and the lower body is now active and the upper body responsive to its lead.

The balance points in the body positions are held in alignment with one another. These points are the balls of the feet, the center of gravity in the lower torso, (navel region), and the ears in the head region. They must remain in alignment with the fixed axis point, the spine, as the club swings around. The eyes remain in a fixed position and work with the balance centers to coordinate each of the working components as the club is swung around the body and out to the intended target.

The five positions in the golf swing

The Five Main Swing Positions

There are Five Main Swing Positions that interact in the motion of the golf swing in this interplay: 1) the Plant or Set-up position; 2) Waist-high with the shoulder-arm triangle intact and the weight and head centered in line behind the ball; 3) the hands and wrists hinged at the top of the swing, and; 4) at Impact with the club squared to the target, and; 5) at Swing's End, which marks the completion of the golf swing.

Set-up Position

Let's examine each of these held positions in the golf swing in more detail (Positions 1–5).

Position 1: The Set-up. The golfer takes a comfortable stance,[8] feet shoulder-width apart, shoulders relaxed, with club in hand. He now extends the club outwards towards the ball, and proceeds to bend from the waist and hips and lowers himself towards the ball, allowing the club to reach close to the ground. He now adds flex with his knees and brings the club directly behind the ball.

The Set-up postion to the ball

8. stance: the standing position of the body to the ball and target.

23

The club rests lightly behind the ball and the left arm is in line with the ball at address. The arms are relaxed and hang comfortably down from his side towards the ball. The golfer's set-up should feel planted in an athletic position and readied to make a swing motion.

Takeaway

Position 2: The golfer swings the club back to a position about waist-high (Position 2). This is done by getting the left shoulder, arm and knee to swing the club back together with the center in a one-piece takeaway. In taking the club back in the backswing, the left arm is predominant and leading as the right arms folds in closer to the right side. The right hand is now cocked at this position.

Swing Thought: Concentrate on taking the club back low and slow. The backswing at this point should feel as if the upper body (shoulders and hips) is making a rotary motion, turning around the spine. The weight shifts or transfers as a result of this action to the inside of the right leg. You should feel your body begin to coil.

The takeaway

24

Top of the Swing

Position 3: The club is swung to the top of the swing. The shoulders and torso continue the rotation of the upper body around the axis point of the spine as the hips and legs now become active in the coiling of the upper body against the resistance of the lower body platform.

Swing Thought: The backswing is primarily an upper body movement away from the ball with the hands following the lead of the arms and shoulders. As the club reaches the top of the swing around ear-level, the lower body becomes active and begins to initiate the move back to the ball. The weight begins to shift and turn the hips towards the left side. This action allows the right side to begins its powerful drive towards the left side and ball at impact position (Position 4).

Swing Thought: As the club is reaching the top of the backswing, the legs get moving towards the ball and the golfer drives his lower body (hips, thighs and knees) into the shot as the club is swung back to the ball.

At the top of the backswing

25

Impact Position

Position 4: Impact. The lower body continues its drive toward the left side and ball as the clubhead and hands lag behind. The momentum of the swinging club and centrifugal force of gravity whip the clubhead at the ball as the hands catch up and release the club into the shot at impact. The club at impact (Position 4) should mirror the golfer's set-up (Position 1) to the ball with the head steady, left arm in line with the club shaft, right arm almost fully extended with the right elbow close to the right hip, and the golfer's center of balance returned to the same point of address at the ball.

Swing's End

Position 5: Swing's End. The body continues to turn with the head still steady in its impact position. The upper part of the left arm is close to the chest. The golfer's body faces the target, completing its rotation, with the majority of the weight on on the left leg. The head moves up now to see the flight of the shot to the

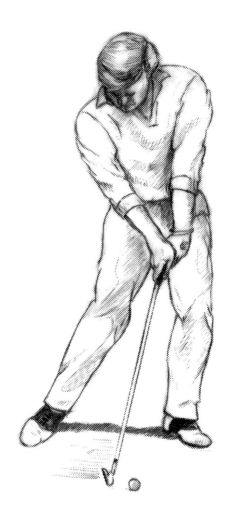

Impact position in the golf swing

target. The right arm is fully extended and the left elbow is folded downward.

The swing comes to rest with the golfer's follow through in which the the left elbow is now away from his side supporting the club and his right arm is extended across his chest. The golfer is facing the target in a balanced position.

The golfer should pay particular attention to how each of these positions work, interact and affect each other. Become more aware of how these motions work and respond to each other in your swing. Practice swinging to each of these positions and linking them together in a continuous manner. Do this on an ongoing basis to groove in the swing.

In the motion of the golf swing, there are two main actions that must occur: balancing of the moving of the center (torso) back and through and the rotation of the arm swing. These actions are constant and in a continuous interaction of held positions from the start of the swing to its completion. Timing of the swing and its execution brings about a heightened sense of awareness of this interplay of motion.

The purpose of the backswing is to create a windup of potential energy that can be quickly transferred to the forward swing to hit

Golfer finishing the swing

27

the ball.

The forward swing's role is to transfer that buildup and release the drive in a fast whip-like accelerating movement at the ball and up against the held left-side position or "wall."

Maximum clubhead speed is reached when the golf swing has gone through each of these held positions and achieves an optimum timing of motion and hinging effect. This creates leverage between the upper and lower body positions as each component interacts, switching roles in the back and forward swings to the target.

The good player learns to use balance and centrifugal force to bring about this interchange and relies on his sense of timing in his attempt to "displace" the left side held position. Each golfer has a limit as to how fast he can generate clubhead speed and hit the ball without losing balance and control in hitting the golf ball. Good players reach well over 100 miles per hour in their swings.

The golfer can drill[9] each of these positions and should do so in developing an effective, powerful swing. Any failure to generate power in the golf swing will emanate from one or more of these areas causing a breakdown where the golfer did not keep a connection and didn't hold a position intact. Free-swinging[10] the club is a good drill to use, to spot check one's positions throughout the swing back and through to the target.

The Interplay of Held Positions Drill

Purpose: To develop the sense of power in the golf swing. The golfer learns that power is generated from the lower body on up, from the feet, legs, through the torso, and transmitted out to the arms and hands. That power in the golf swing is regulated by the center of the body in the driving action of the pivot and thrust at the ball. The golfer learns to integrate the driving action of the body with the momentum of motion (gravity and centrifugal force) in the golf swing to cause, create leverage and optimum clubhead speed.

Emphasis: The objective of this drill is learning where your power source lies, which is your center and use of balance. In order to do this you

9. drill: a training exercise
10. free-swinging: making a practice swing back and forth without the ball

need to develop a sense of feel, of how the rotation of the body and the arm swing coordinate and work together in the swing.

Part I: Free-swing the club back and through. Notice how the rotation of the body moves best with the club. Notice how moving from your center, which is your balance point, regulates the arm swing and rotation of the body, and additionally dictates the timing pattern in your swing. These two motions (the arm swing and the rotation of the body) need to feel connected and be working together.

Part II: What you want to further groove in here is the interaction of the arm swing and motion of the torso (stomach, back and hips) in a one piece swing. In this part of the drill work on sweeping the club back and through utilizing the torso as a unit. Think of moving your navel out of the way going back and turning it back through the ball.

The golf swing becomes the "hooking up" or connective feeling of both the arm swing and body not only working together, but also releasing together at impact. This is the most effective position to work the swing. It can be perfected by learning to move from your center (balance point) and developing a keener sense of timing and using

The golfer moving from his center and maintaining balance. This creates leverage and power in the swing

29

centrifugal force, which when swung correctly will instinctively "cue" when to drive and release the club into the ball at the moment of impact.

Now the lower body acts as a base that stabilizes as a platform position, starting with the feet position (the weight on the balls of the feet) evenly distributed and aligned with the legs, hips, and shoulders in that order on up to the head. This position allows the optimum transference of energy generated from the ground up from the resistance of both the upper and lower body positions.

Part III: Swing the club back to each of the Five Positions (Set-up, Waist-High, Top of the Backswing, Impact, and Swing's End). Now swing the club back and through in a continuous manner observing the interaction between the arm swing and the trunk of the body. Now get the feeling of the torso and arms working together as the club is swung back and forth.

The objective here is to get the swing and body rotation working together in a coordinated effort that times the release into the ball at the right time. Coordination of these positions and movements is the timing of the interplay, which allows the ball to be struck in the most optimum manner.

End Result: A golfer who has a better awareness of the swing's motion, its interplay of held positions, and can make a powerful golf swing.

The Importance of Balance

Balance is an important component here and needs to be kept constant and become second nature, yet it is something that the good player constantly monitors for correct feel and position in the mechanics of the swing. Continue to make swings to the point that the interaction of each held position leads to the other and you are more confident with the swing's operation. Make this part of your daily routine. This is something that you can do without the ball by just free swinging the club back and forth through each of the key swing positions. Use of a mirror helps you see this interaction.

Chapter III

Transfer of Energy in the Golf Swing

The golf swing is the result of a series of chain-like reactions in which energy is transmitted into power at the moment of impact. The mass of the clubhead combines with hand speed and the flexing of the shaft to accelerate this transfer of energy in hitting the ball. This happens in about a second and a half!

It was observed in the golf swings of advanced players that they work the swing from the bottom up, from the feet, leveraging the lower body position of the hips, legs and feet together to obtain maximum clubhead speed at the ball in the forward swing. All good ball strikers have good footwork and shift their weight back and through to the ball and target. It is this timely motion with the feet and lower body that brings about this transfer of energy and clubhead speed.

In contrast to this, the higher handicap golfer hasn't yet learned to use the position correctly to drive the clubhead into the ball with the lower body. He is relying instead on more of the upper body strength in the arms and shoulders in the swing, throwing the upper body into the shot at the wrong time. In doing so a good turn or coil cannot be properly effected, thus robbing the swing of harnessing any real potential power. This causes a premature release and definite loss of power.

Good footwork is an essential component in this transfer of energy in the successful golf swing. Many of the great ball strikers of the game were known for their excellent sense of timing with their footwork in a back and through, dance like, rhythmic motion. Sam Snead, Lee Trevino, and Billy Casper are excellent examples of working the swing from the ground up with their "poetry in motion" movement with the feet. Footwork is the dance-step of the golf swing.

Chapter IV

Power in the Golf Swing

Good strikers of the ball work the legs, thighs, hips, and feet into the shot. The hips initiate the movement into the ball. This is both a lateral[11] and rotary movement in which the golfer drives the lower body (thighs, knees, legs and feet) into the shot. The torso and shoulders of the upper body follow in the sequence, as power in the golf swing is transferred out through the arms and hands to the club and ball at impact.

The club acts as an extension of the arm and hands as it hits the ball. This is evident in the swing of all good players. Jack Nicklaus, Sam Snead, Tom Watson, Bobby Jones, and Walter Hagen are excellent examples of power in the golf swing in their movement back to the ball.

In a research study done in 1986 by Centinela Hospital Medical Center at its sports medicine and biomechanics[12] lab, the swings of

Powerful drive into the ball at impact position

11. lateral: sideways
12. biomechanics; the study of the interactions of the body, its stress points, and the rotation of the golf swing through space and accelerated force in hitting the ball

33

professional golfers were compared with those of various amateur golfers. The purpose of this three-year study was to compile information for a program that golfers could follow to reduce risk of injury, improve timing and overall performance in their games.

Their independent study confirms this notion in the transfer of energy of the swing—that power in golf comes sequentially from the feet up as you rotate your body into the shot. Energy is transferred starting from the legs through the hips to the upper trunk, then to the shoulders and out through the arms to the wrists and hands and finally to the club itself.[13]

Power in the golf swing does not derive from a forceful movement in trying to "muscle" the shot to its target as many golfers attempt to do. It depends chiefly on the timing of the rotation of the lower body: the hips and thighs are the strongest generators of power in the body and drive into the ball. The hands and clubhead accelerate and whip through the shot at impact and out towards the target.

One of the chief difficulties that the golfer has to deal with stems not from making the actual swing but from initiating or starting the golf swing. This is a problem of some magnitude for most golfers.

Unlike other sports that use a club, racquet or bat and provide the necessary stimulus in which the player responds to the incoming ball, golf, being an individual game, requires the golfer to hit the ball from a static or still position. This permits the player to think or deliberate too much over the ball which usually results in a "mental freeze," and produces a rigid, mechanical attempt at making the golf swing.

Many a golfer finds himself thinking so hard trying to avoid doing the wrong things in the swing and getting everything just right that he gets into a "paralysis by analysis," —an introverted state of mind instead of sticking to one or two "swing keys" or fundamentals and just concentrating on making good contact and hitting the ball to the target.

The pro and good player of the game—knowing the importance of getting the swing going without thinking too much over the ball—will work a pattern into their pre-shot routines, a "waggle" of the club such as Ben Hogan's, a pre-cock of the head of Jack Nicklaus, a preset of the right knee of Gary Player, a slight rocking left of center and back of Greg Norman, a

---

13. "30 Exercises to Better Golf," by Frank W. Jobe, M.D. and Diane R. Moynes, M.S., R.P.T., Centinella Hospital Medical Center

slight set of the hips as Curtis Strange does, or any one or combinations of these to activate their swings to the target. One of these routines may be the right "lever" just for you in your game.

The Backswing

The backswing is essentially a potential setup or preparatory action that sets the stage for the shot to come, the forward swing to the ball and its intended target. It is ideally initiated by a lever or "swing key"[14] as discussed above and sweeps the club back, pulling the heel of the left foot off the ground as the club is swung around the axis point (the spine) to the top of the swing, where now the hands and wrists are hinged, fully cocked and readied for their release through the ball at impact.

During this process the weight has been transferred from the middle of the body to the back (right) leg via the golfer's center of gravity. This reaches Swing Positions 2 and 3 at waist level and at the top of the backswing.

The trunk of the upper body along with the arms and shoulders rotate around a fixed central axis—the spine and the head—achieving a coiled position at the top of the swing. This is accomplished in the following approximate ratio of rotation: shoulders 90%, hips 60–75%, and knees 25–40%, but will vary with each player due to their degree of flexibility and strength.

There is an additional axis point that sets up in the backswing in the lower right leg position extending from the ball of the foot up the leg to the knee that is important, as it acts as a position "holder" for the weight once transferred on the backswing and also in creating resistance to the swing's coil. It is in direct line with the right hip and will feel connected.

The upper body is coiled against the lower body platform which creates the necessary resistance in the building up of potential energy and power in the golf swing. Without this "held position," the golfer develops a sway and can't get into position to drive down and into the ball at impact.

This axis point will move to the same position on the left side and leg as the forward swing seeks impact and hits up against this point on the left side. It is also important to note that once the club is released at the ball the

14. swing key: a thought, idea or swing motion that the golfer uses to "key" his swing

left arm and its connection to the chest allow a hinging effect to take place in the follow-through to the swing's completion. This is another reason that balance and keeping the head steady at impact are so important in golf.

A whole book having to do with the importance of staying connected in the golf swing was written by Jim Ballard, entitled *How To Perfect Your Golf Swing*. He makes a very good point about this and helped shape Hal Sutton's game and refined Curtis Strange's swing in the early 1980s.

Ballard stated, "...the idea of connection became the master fundamental. It was not at all complicated, and I didn't really consider it as either theory or concept. It was an observable physical reality—what was actually happening in the best golf swings. Initially, connection was made up of grip, position, and balance, and a connected golf swing possessed all of the common denominators—the essential fundamentals."[15]

Too many golfers have become so absorbed in their thinking of mechanics and swing plane that they forget that it is the intention to make an efficient swing based on feel that counts in hitting the ball to the target.

It is this above principle that aligns or ties together the mechanics of the golf swing and those of movement. All the great players of the game, past and present, have mastered its principle.

Just as the golf club is balanced in such a way to make it possible to swing the clubhead around the body to achieve maximum clubhead speed, the golfer must be "rooted" and balanced not just from bottom to top, feet to head and vice versa—but connected through the center of his body—in order to achieve the optimum rotation and its product of maximum transference of potential energy in the golf swing at impact.

15. *How To Perfect Your Golf Swing*, by Jim Ballard

The upper body and being connected throughout the golf swing
as shown by Tom Watson

Chapter V

Three Key Fundmentals:
Grip, Stance and Alignment

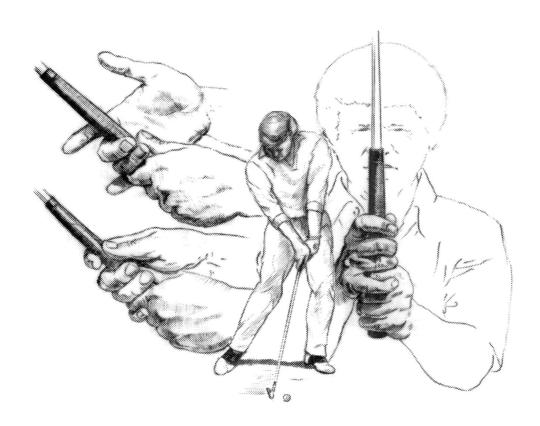

The hands and the grip working in the swing

The golf swing is built around three key Outer Game fundamentals: Grip, Stance, and Alignment. Each of these components and their interrelated functions must work together as a unit or system in the golf swing.

A good grip is a vital foundation in the golf swing. All good ball-striking is the coordinated action of the hands and body working together in a harmonious flow of movement.

As we will discuss further in this section in regards to feel (Chapter IX, The Sensory Feel System in Golf), the player's only direct physical contact with the club and ball is through the clubhead via his hands. In the golf swing, the power is derived from and generated by the movements of the body. As this power builds up, there is a transference of energy from the body to the arms and from there to the clubhead.

The hands whip through the shot in a tremendous chain reaction. This reaction depends on a proper grip. With an improper golf grip, this chain of events with the swing and body can't take place effectively.

Types of Grips

The overlapping grip is the standard grip used by the majority of players. This is the Vardon grip, named after Harry Vardon, who made it popular in Great Britain and America. The interlocking and ten finger or "baseball grip" round out the basic type of grips used by golfers; 90% of all golfers use the overlapping grip. The interlocking grip appeals to golfers, who have shorter, stubbier fingers. Jack Nicklaus is the best example of a player who uses it.

Different grips are used in more variety around and on the green, in chipping and in putting than anywhere else. There are plenty of variations used by golfers on the greens. Feel and consistency have all to do with the type of grip chosen by the player.

The key element in the golf grip is that both hands are working together as a synchronized unit. This is all important.

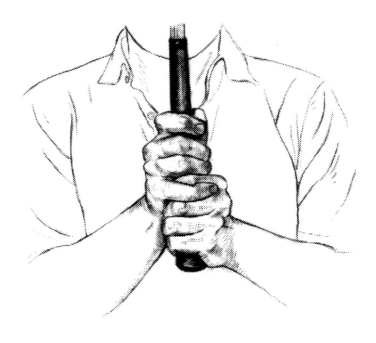

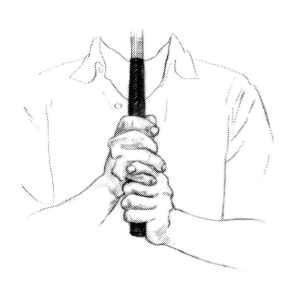

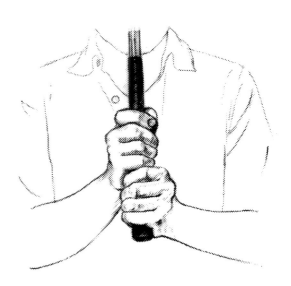

The different types of grip: Overlapping, Interlocking, and Baseball grips

Grip Pressure

The grip is threaded between the fingers, and the palm of the hand in the left hand grip. The back three fingers of the left hand receive more pressure and are firm on the club. The right hand is placed on the club in the fingers as opposed to in the palm of the left hand. This is important.

The pressure points are in the two middle fingers of the right hand. The thumb and index finger of the right hand are lightly touching together, forming a V in the direction of the right shoulder.

These are the "trigger" fingers that control the fine sensitivity of feel and control, that assist in hitting down and through the shot, and in putting spin on the ball, especially on the shorter iron and pitch shots.

One should guard against the grip being too rigid as this robs the sense of feel in the hands, and the natural action of the hinging of the wrists. The club should feel as if you were holding onto it just enough to prevent it from slipping out of or turning in your hands in response to someone holding the other end of it. Strive for a grip pressure that's comfortable, but firm in your hands.

You can drill the above with your own grip in the following manner.

 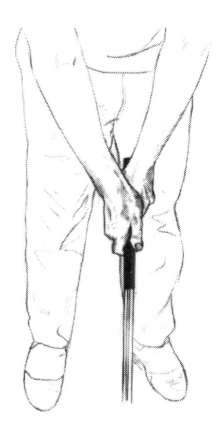

The Vs of the left and right hand grip position

THE GOLF GRIP DRILL

Purpose: To determine the correct grip pressure in the golf swing.

Emphasis: This drill is rather elementary, yet gets the point across about correct grip pressure. It's done with another golfer, who holds the opposite end of a golf club in his hands. The golfer takes hold of the grip portion of the club as the club is held out for him to take. He positions both his hands on the club as in taking his golf grip in a firm enough manner so that the club doesn't twist, turn, or drop from his hands as the other golfer continues to hold onto the club from the other end.

By exerting too much firmness, the golfer finds the grip becomes too tense and rigid to hold onto, and in gripping too light, the grip becomes too slack while held from the other end by the coach, who then could easily twist the club around.

In addition to this drill, one can do the following exercise to get his grip pressure correct: Take your normal grip and place the club in the following three positions: on the ground, parallel to the ground, and vertical. Notice how the club feels in each of these positions, being either too heavy to support in the arms when held parallel, or too light when held above. The golfer will find that the grip pressure feels right in his hands when the club is gripped and held at a forty-five degree angle, which is either about two feet below or above waist level. This is the correct amount of firmness for the grip.

From this position the golfer lowers his hands, bending slightly from the knees and waist, to his setup position with the arms hanging down and in, just behind the ball.

End Result: A golfer who knows, and has the correct grip pressure worked out in his grip.

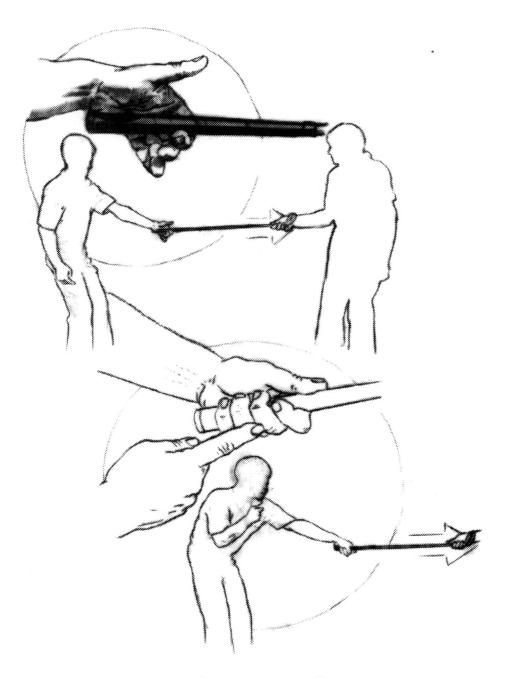

Correct pressure in the golf grip

45

Stance and Alignment

The proper stance and alignment to the ball and target enable the golfer to be in an athletic position and balanced throughout the swing. Positioned correctly, the legs, hips, and body can function and carry out their true role in the golf swing, and thus bring about good golf shots. Alignment to the ball is critical in the outcome of hitting golf shots on line to the target.

Faulty alignment, aiming too far right or left of the target, can cause the shot to consistently miss the mark, even when struck well. This can lead to a variety of errors, and can compound problems with the swing that can be

The stance for the woods

The stance for the irons

46

one of the main reasons for the player not playing to his potential in the Outer Game. The stance is positioned in the following manner: on woods and long irons, the feet are placed shoulder-length apart, with the weight on the middle to the ball of the foot. The feet are spread farther apart on the driver, but watch for the stance becoming too wide as this restricts the action of the turn in the windup. The weight is distributed a little more on the right side of the body on these shots, between 55–60%.

Progressing into the irons, the stance becomes shorter, as the golfer uses the mid irons, from the six iron on down to the wedge. The weight becomes more on the left side of the body, about 55–60% as well.

How you set up and align yourself to the target is of chief importance in the Outer Game approach. The ideal position that the golfer needs to be in is an athletic position, on balance and readied to set the swing motion going to the target. The body should feel that it is in a "braced connected position" with the arms, shoulder, and center forming a triangle, and parallel to the target. More on this later in this section.

The ideal position of stance and alignment

The Law of Centering in the Golf Swing

The golf swing is swung around the spine. In doing so, the swing forms an ellipse[16] The arms swing up and around more in a vertical position, whereas the body rotates around the spine in a horizontal plane. Imagine the arm swing as the vertical, up and down motion of a ferris wheel in its revolution, and the rotation of the body in a merry-go-round motion as it goes around.

The swing forming a circle. Note example of the vertical and horizontal planes of the ferris wheel and merry-go-rounds.

16. ellipse: an oval having both ends alike

The whole trick is to coordinate the interaction of both of these motions into a synchronized, one piece flowing movement. The swing is worked from the center or balance point of the body and must utilize this principle in order to hit the ball efficiently.

Centering is a principle applied to movement here in golf derived from its use and application in Eastern philosophy and the martial arts in working the mind and body as a unit and in the release in striking or blocking a blow. This is something which that I have been intrigued with and have studied as a student for some years when I did Thai Chi Chuan back in Chicago, where I saw it for the first time. This martial art form blends a harmony of power, aesthetics, graceful flow, and mental discipline.

It is used by a number of athletes in their training to foster better concentration and conditioning. I have read that several women players on the LPGA have used it in their golf to improve their flexibility and ability to concentrate.

From this study, I have incorporated this principle into a workable form of movement in the golf swing that is actually a move that all good players use. It hasn't been identified as a fundamental in the teaching of the golf swing before now. To illustrate this point, let's take the golf club for example and have you balance it on your index finger as an exercise of this principle—in order to do so since the clubhead is the heaviest part of the club, you have to hold it closer to the clubhead in order to balance it properly. This point is its center of gravity.

If you took just the shaft and nothing else you would find that the center of the shaft is its balance point and center of gravity and you balance it rather easily. Well, the same holds true for the positioning and balancing of the body.

The body's center of gravity and balance point is in the center closer to the upper point of the hips (or below the navel in the front) and the lower point of the back muscles above the tail bone of the body.

There is a law that encompasses this in movement and applies to the golf swing.

**ALL WELL EXECUTED GOLF SHOTS ARE THE RESULT OF MOTION
FROM THE GOLFER'S CENTER OF GRAVITY OR BALANCE POINT
IN THE HITTING OF THE BALL.**

All well executed shots are the result of motion from the golfer's center of gravity or balance point in the hitting of the golf ball.

Chapter VI

Gravity—May The Force Be With You In Golf

Any discussion concerning the golf swing and its laws of mechanics and movement would be incomplete without taking up the principle that I call Gravity Golf and the Leverage Game.

The golf swing requires precise timing of its components all working together in a synergy[17] of movement to produce a well executed swing. All principles of movement in any athletic endeavor derive from a basic understanding and observation of the laws of physics; particularly those of motion and force and its relationship with objects. This is where the physical laws of gravity, centrifugal force and momentum come into play.

An understanding of these principles, especially those of centrifugal force and momentum and how to apply them to golf will be found by the golfer to be the common denominator in the execution of the swing. This is Timing.

The golf swing is connected up by a series of levers of a fixed length (skeletal bones) and pivots (joints) that are connected in the upper and lower body segments with a fixed center—the spine, which is the pivot of the body. Thus we have an assembly of levers and pivots that must work together as a unit with the spine. Muscles are flexors acting in a resilient way, to not only hold this whole assembly together, but to generate the needed strength and power to the swing.

As the golfer swings the club back and around the body these levers and pivots go into action as a systematic unit, and create a leverage effect with the club and body in an interplay of held positions and motions. This lever assembly system is two-part: the upper body (arms and shoulders) and the lower body (the golf club, hands, and wrists).

17. synergy: the mutual action of two or more substances working together to achieve an effect

51

LEVER

PIVOT

Golfer pivoting around the spine. Note the lever and pivot

The spine is the pivot of the body. In golf it serves as the central axis point[18] around which the club and body follow a prescribed, circular path. The club as it is swung around the body gains speed, thus creating centrifugal force causing the force that drives the clubhead to pull outward, away from its center or axis point, and thus accelerate speed as the club approaches its point of release at the ball.

The platform position of the lower body holds its position and resists the tendency of the club to move outward, the rotation of the torso (especially the hips) acts to "flatten" or straighten out the club's path as the arms and hands naturally begin to cross over at the ball with the club face now squared at impact position.

18. axis point: the reference point around which the swing revolves

Centrifugal forces in the golf swing. Notice (a) the tendency of the club to move outward in the swing phase to the target and (b) the role of the torso in resisting this force

In the forward swing to the target the lower body position quickly gains momentum and becomes the dominant force in accelerating the clubhead in whip-like fashion towards impact at the ball.

The arm swing cannot be allowed to predominate or be too wristy in the golf swing. It has to follow the dictate of the movement of the body's center which determines not only the correct address position for a given shot, but also the necessary amount of arm and clubhead speed to support its rotation in achieving maximum acceleration with the clubhead.

This is why it is very important to pay particular attention to your set-up[19] position to the ball on all shots in the alignment phase as you want to work with the gravity, not against it. Looking the shot over gives the golfer his first impression at this factor and will affect the resultant swing plane position throughout the swing.

19. set-up: the alignment to the ball and target by the club and body

Centrifugal force at work in the forward swing phase of the hammer-thrower and the golfer

Spine Angle

Proper position to the ball, (Position 1), especially spine angle is important and needs to be kept constant in the rotation of the body in hitting the ball. This is especially true where you encounter uneven lies and terrain and in these cases the golfer needs to calculate this effect, and build in a compensating factor in the swing via the weight distribution to counteract its influence. Where this angle varies, a misalignment with the spine and hips in the lower body and torso in the upper body positions results in an inconsistent swing plane and shots.

Spine angle and proper position to the ball

The rule of thumb that I give here is to put added weight on the side of the spine and foot that is either uphill (left side) or downhill (right side) of the target.

Gravity and the Golf Swing

Gravity is a factor that affects not only sports but every sense of movement as we know it in life. It is basic in how we walk and move as human beings. It becomes something of "second nature" to all of us in our daily lives but is not actually fully understood by many golfers in its role and interaction in their playing the game.

Since gravity is constant and most predictable, it makes good sense to build arm and club speed around it. Clubhead speed depends totally on the coordination of the sum of the component parts in the golf swing. Golfers "break the law" when they exceed clubhead speed limits, where they try to force the acceleration of the combined arm swing and upper body strength to overpower the shot in the swing. To apply this principle, do the following drill.

GETTING GRAVITY TO WORK IN THE GOLF SWING DRILL

Purpose: To attain a working understanding of how gravity (and centrifugal force) works in the golf swing. This has to do with developing the proper sense of timing of the swing's rotation: the arm swing, clubhead, and body. Let's first look at how gravity comes into play in the swing.

Emphasis: This drill deals with the various elements in the swing that are affected by motion and the resistance that is brought about by the interplay of held positions. It also teaches the necessary timing pattern that all good swingers have in their game.

Part I: The golfer lets his arms hang down comfortably from his side. He assumes his stance, bending some from the knees and hips. His feet are close together about six to eight inches apart as if he was hitting or pitching a nine iron or wedge shot. He swings back and through without a club, noticing how easy the arms move from the shoulder back and through in the motion of the swing.

The golfer can vary the width of his stance a bit, placing his feet and knees closer together or wider. From this position he swings his arms supported by the movement of his torso back and through in a practice swing a number of times.

Notice how from this position the swing has to be made from the arms and shoulders and has to be supported by the torso, mainly from the center of the body in an effort to balance and time the swing's rotation. The arms and hands swing are synchronizes to this rotation as the club is swung back and forth in the swing.

The golfer is to put more attention on the swing moving from the center of his body. This is done by having him move from his mid-section or navel as the arm swing rotates around the spine or pivot in the takeaway and back through in the forward motion. These elements must work with, not against the force of gravity.

Part II: In this part of the drill, the golfer now places his arms across his chest in a criss-cross position. He is to then makes a series of practice swings back and through from this position (without a club). The golfer is to notice how the upper body regulates, and "hooks up" the rotation of the arm and body in a one piece movement to the top of the backswing. The rotation of both the arms and body should feel synchronized, and well-timed.

Now using a club, the golfer swings the club back and forth, keying on the image of this swing motion, and its sense of feel. This feel sensation is to be worked into the swing.

Part III: Now the golfer with a club assumes his normal stance for a wood or long iron and with arms hanging down comfortably at his side, he works on coordinating the rotation of the arm swing and the body. The backswing should feel as if the golfer is linking up these held positions, one by one, into a powerful coil at the top of the backswing in a well-balanced, readied for release at the ball and target. The key to this part of the drill is to focus on coordinating the swing's rotation—moving the club (arms and shoulders) and body back together as one and through to the target.

End Result: A golfer who, by effectively coordinating the arm and body rotation, can make gravity work for him as a powerful force in the golf swing.

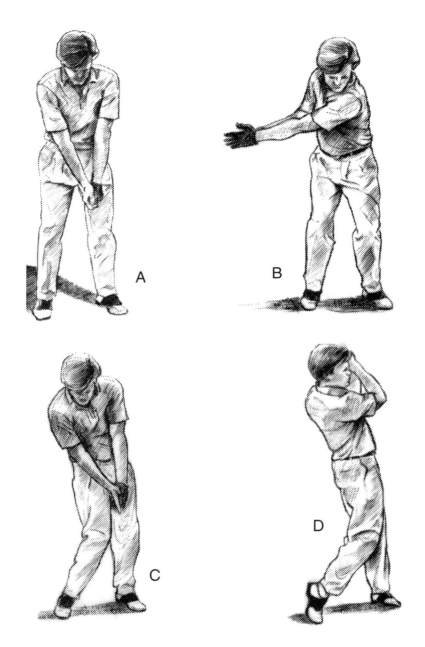

A: Golfer assumes stance letting his arms hang down comfortably from his side and bends from the knees and hips. Feet are placed together as if pitching a nine iron or wedge shot;

B,C and D: golfer makes a series of practice swings back and through noticing how easy the arms and shoulders move in the motion of the swing

A   B   C

The golfer now places his arms across his chest in a criss-cross position. He then makes a series of similar practice swings as in Drill I back and through from this position without a club and then repeats this part of the drill with a club. If the golfer has done the previous drill correctly, he should sense the linking or "hooking-up" of the torso and arm swings working together in the swing as he swings back and forth

Now in regards to the other force, centrifugal force, I've included the following drill that will help groove in this component in your swing.

If the golfer has done the previous drill correctly, he should sense the linking or "hooking-up" of the torso and arm swings working together in the swing as he swings back and forth.

CENTRIFUGAL FORCE DRILL

Purpose: To understand how centrifugal force works in the golf swing and how to use it.

Emphasis: Swing the club back and through, along a similar path of that of a baseball swing (a horizontal plane), paying particular attention to how the clubhead first lags behind the pull of the hands and arms as the club is swung around the body. Get the feel of the club returning to the ball in the forward swing as it picks up momentum and attempts to move momentarily outward, away from the center of the body's rotation to the target.

Notice how the hips in the forward swing to the target, having driven towards the ball and the left side position, "put on the brakes," as the hands and wrists catch up and release the club into the ball in a whip-like, accelerating fashion. This is centrifugal force in the golf swing.

Make about five or ten swings back and forth in an effort to get the sensation of the speed of the clubhead moving outward in the forward swing. Allow the wrists to cock going back, release, and cross over in the forward swing in the swing to the target.

Now swing the club back and forth like this but on a lower horizontal plane, closer to that of your own swing, grooving-in the feel of the club picking up speed at the bottom of the arc as the clubhead is whipped into the ball. Notice how the club picks up speed in its rotation towards the ball at the bottom of the swing's path and is moving outward away from the body towards the right of the target as it approaches impact position.

End Result: A golfer who can make centrifugal force work for him in the golf swing.

The golfer (a) at waist level position with club in hand holding a triangle position between the arms, club and waist, (b) the drive in the forward swing as the hands whip the club through to the intended target and club moves outward to the target

Hooking up and Connecting the Swing

The golf swing consisting of the upper and lower body movement needs to be worked from the center in order to "hook up" these two components to work effectively together as a unit. The swing becomes a feeling of "hooking up" or "connecting up" the upper and lower body segments and its center. The proper feel in the swing is with the body making the move away from the ball and back through to the ball—as opposed to the hands leading the way in the swing motion.

The golfer "hooking up" the upper and lower body positions via the center of the body and working the rotation of the swing as a unit

The only time that this changes is on the shorter irons from about the seven iron down through the wedge. This is primarily due to the shorter lengths of the club, which alter the plane into a more vertical position. The center of gravity moves correspondingly higher on shorter shots in the positioning of the body.

One of the problems with golf instruction is the lack of a complete understanding of what the golfer is trying to do with the golf swing and shot. There is a lack of integration between these two areas with too much attention having been placed on the swing and its mechanics. Even today very few instructors understand the function of the dynamics of motion and movement in the golf swing.

High speed computer analysis has created a whole field called biomechanics which has emerged to provide studies of the body in motion to fill this gap between mechanics and the principles of movement. Conventional golf instruction over the last several decades has continued to place ninety-five percent of its teaching on the mechanics of the golf swing and the intricacies of its techniques.

When a subject becomes too ridden with theories and individual opinions of what's right and what isn't, then that pursuit has become too complex and difficult to understand in its basic principles and has "lost" its basic truths. This is such the case with the swing today in the game of golf.

There is too much theory having to do with mechanics, especially in the articles of golf magazines and books that abound today. This confuses even a number of pros. Beyond the fundamental principles of the golf swing, technique becomes individualized with each golfer as each develops a style often with its own peculiarities.

Unfortunately technique has become the watchword and emphasis in instruction, yet the learning of the golf swing has developed into an explanation of the effects or consequences of the golf swing, not the causes or function of such. "Looking up," "you didn't keep your head down," are not the reasons for the mis-hit shot but the effect of a more basic reason or cause.

This leads to a misidentification of the actual cause of a poorly played golf shot leaving the golfing student with the idea now that he must "keep the head still at all times" or similar notion in the golf swing. Several weeks and months later, the golfer has worked his swing into a pronounced reverse pivot[20] from such instruction that now needs correction and undoing.

The previous drills provide an understanding of the laws of the movement and the necessary components of a successful swing!

---

20. reverse pivot: incorrect turn in which too much weight is on the left side

Chapter VII

The Natural Laws of Movement in Golf

There are four key fundamentals in the movement of the golf swing. These are: BALANCE, RHYTHM, TEMPO, and TIMING. They are the building blocks of an efficient golf swing and must work together, in order to master the game of golf. Without them or with one or more of these components weak, the others are affected in the quality and workability of the golf shot. They comprise the Natural Laws of Movement in the Golf Swing and are oddly enough not well understood in the swings of the majority of golfers.

A full understanding of how each of these components functions in the swing will build the proper foundation upon which the technique of hitting a golf shot can be fully learned.

As a matter of fact, in the research that I conducted with the basics of movement, it was found one for one to be the area that held each golfer back from mastering the mechanics of the golf swing and playing to his full potential. The basics of movement turned out to be the *missing link* in instruction with students.

Understanding and application has to be built upon a gradient of steps in order for true learning to take place. Good players have learned the NAT-URAL LAWS OF MOVEMENT and can thus concentrate their attention on the mental aspects of the game. Technique beyond the fundamentals becomes the individual domain of style of the player. That is all there is to it. So just learn the fundamentals and let your own style come about.

No two golfers swing alike, yet in all good players you'll see the mastery of these laws of movement working in a smooth transition, the correct sequencing of the upper body in the backswing with the lower body in the forward swing as the golfer synchronizes these actions into a one-piece movement in hitting the ball.

The Cycle of Action

Each time that you hit a golf shot to its target you are in essence following a natural law in the physical universe. You are performing a cycle of action.

A Cycle of Action[21] is an action that starts, changes, and then comes to a stop or completion point. A golf shot is envisioned in the mind as what the golfer wants to have happen—this is the start of the cycle of action and is then formulated into the right swing that will produce the intended result—the change phase, and is then brought to completion, the shot has now been

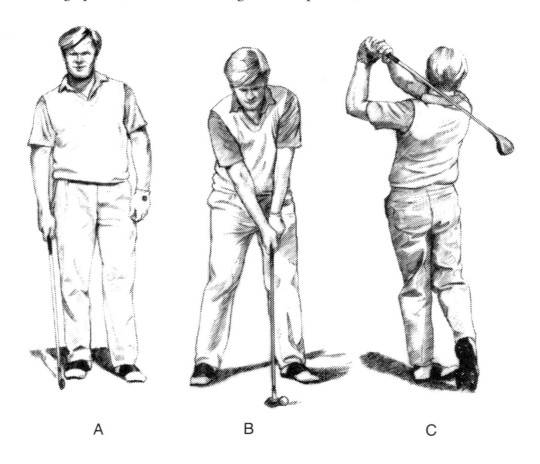

A   B   C

The Cycle of Action in hitting a golf shot: A) Start: the pre-shot routine and alignment, B) Change: hitting or execution of the shot and C) Stop: finish of the swing

21. Cycle of Action: from the book, *Problems of Work,* by L. Ron Hubbard

hit to the target—its completion point. So what we have in the cycle of action is a Start—Change—Completion pattern in every golf shot that one hits.

The golfer has an intention to hit the ball from Point "A" over a distance to a target, let's say here to Point "B." This cycle occurs within a finite period of time, say about sixty seconds from its onset.

One of the main problems that the golfer is faced with that differs from other sports is that the golfer has to start the cycle of action in golf from a "static"[22] or still position alongside of the ball. It's up to him to initiate the cycle of action in the swing each time in making the shot, getting it started, continuing it and then bringing it to its completion. This can and does present a problem for the golfer as he has to start the motion going whereas in tennis, baseball, and other racquet sports the ball provides the stimulus to the player each time.

In order to hit a good golf shot the golfer has to learn to think and "play the piano" in a prescribed manner of "keys" and "notes." The keys are the "movement section" and the notes are the "tempo section." These two "sections" orchestrate or blend into a controlled, timed sequential motion.

Balance in the Golf Swing

Balance is the component that the golfer uses to steady the golf swing on a firm foundation and use gravity and centrifugal force to their fullest in the hitting of the golf shot.

Let's define what Balance is here. The dictionary defines balance as noun: a state of equilibrium, steadiness. As a verb: to bring into or maintain in a state of equilibrium. The word itself is derived from the Latin equilibrium, even balance: equi + libra, balance.

Proper balance is necessary in the golf swing in order to hit a good shot. The degree that balance is off in the swing will reduce the given potential to make a good shot. The other components all hinge on proper balance in hitting a good golf shot to the target.

This brings us to the natural law about balance, that is the cornerstone of movement in the swing:

> ALL WELL EXECUTED GOLF SHOTS ARE THE RESULT OF PROPER BALANCE THROUGHOUT THE GOLF SWING.

22. static: still; at rest; having no motion

Proper balance is necessary in the golf swing

Weight Distribution, Width and Spine Angle

Your balance, how you address the ball, is vitally important in the golf swing. Its importance can not be over emphasized. How you set-up to the ball depends on three chief factors: Weight Distribution, Width, and Spine Angle.

The weight is distributed in the following manner. On long shots, for the woods and irons, the weight is slightly more on the right side of the spine, between fifty to sixty percent. This is in order to promote a better turn and pivot into the right side. The middle irons finds the weight evenly distributed. The short irons have the weight more emphasized on the left side, say between fifty to sixty percent depending on the type of shot encountered.

The golfer at set-up position with balance evenly distributed on both feet with a driver. The illustration shows the proper width of the feet.

The weight always stays on the insides of the feet. A quick study of sports involving swinging a stick, racket or club such as ice hockey or tennis, reveals the weight inside the hips, knees or feet. Such is the case in boxing in which the boxer stays behind his punches and never allows the weight to roll to the outside of their left hip and foot.

The width of the feet should be, as a rule of thumb, about shoulder

69

length apart on the woods and long irons, and becomes progressively shorter as the club decreases in number and length.

How you stand up to the ball determines the angle of the spine from which you swing the club. This directly influences the plane in which the club travels back and forward to the ball. The position of the body, the torso and especially that of the hips, when in proper alignment, fixes the angle of the club shaft to be swung around the body that will return to the ball at optimum angle at impact.

Proper balance can be acquired by doing the following drill.

NATURAL LAWS OF GOLF BALANCE DRILL

Purpose: To teach the golfer the importance of balance and how to use it in the golf swing.

Part I: In the first part of the drill, the golfer learns to set-up to the ball without the club first. He is to walk into the hitting position from behind and to the side of the ball. Then, he's to stand with his shoulders erect and take a stance that's about shoulder-length apart. As he takes his stance, he's to bend from the hips and let his arms hang down by his side.

The weight is concentrated from the middle to the ball of each foot. The hips are tilted slightly forward and aligned a bit to the left with the rear-end slightly out. The head is moved somewhat behind the position of the ball at address with the left eye looking more at the ball. The chin is tucked or positioned a bit downward and holds that position throughout the swing.

Emphasis: The whole idea here is to set-up to the ball in a comfortable, athletic position that is steady, on balance, and readied for movement. The golfer's stance or alignment to the ball should be such that a springiness is felt in the legs and feet as he addresses the ball.

For the purpose of this drill, the golfer has the weight evenly distributed and proceeds to make a series of swings back and throughout, keeping in mind the importance of maintaining balance throughout the swing. He should check his balance at set-up position, at the top of the swing, impact position, and at the completion of the swing.

The golfer will find that the key to being balanced in the golf swing lies in moving the club and body back together. In doing so the center of gravity of the body, just below the beltline at the second sacral segment[23], will align

23. second sacral segment: the balance point or center of gravity of the body

the upper body position, the hub[24] of the swing, with the lower body position in its rotation to the target.[25]

The hub of the swing and its center

24. Hub: the center of a wheel; the point around which the golfer swings the club on an inclined plane
25: *The Physiology of the Joints,* Volume 3 by I.A. Kapandji. [Note: this information provided by Dr. Jeff Blanchard, D.C. and scratch golfer]

The image of a weight lifter, baseball pitcher, or bowler comes to mind as each of these sports require firm balance and moving from the center or balance point of the body.

If you find that you are falling back away from the ball at impact then your balance has been thrown off or not shifted correctly, which will cause a number of other swing related problems.

Part II: In the second part of this drill, the golfer uses the club this time to practice swinging the club on balance.

Picture the toss of a ball to a child. This is a good visual image with regards to footwork in the golf swing

Set-up to the ball in the above described manner with the athletic position at address. Place the club beside and behind the ball. Swing the club back and through maintaining your balance throughout the swing. Make sure that the weight is between the middle and ball of the foot area. In the proper address position, the body will feel connected, grounded, and readied for action.

The golfer swings back from his center, allowing the weight to shift to the back leg in a continuous one piece action. Don't rush or jerk the club or the weight shift back on the backswing. Work on timing the release of the shot in the downswing.

The golf shot is worked from the ground up starting with the feet. Good footwork is important as the feet provide the feel of the ground as you swing back and through. They provide sensory input and feedback to the body's sensory feel system.

The use of a mirror is helpful in this drill as it allows you to see how you're swinging and maintaining balance. This is something that one can do at the course, home, out on the porch. Also, you can check your swing in the reflection of a window.

Check your balance on a regular basis yourself, or with the watchful eye of your golf instructor, or one of your golfing buddies. Don't underestimate the importance of balance in the swing. It's one of the constant checkpoints that the pros monitor all the time.

End Result: A golfer who sets up to the shot on balance and can maintain that balance throughout the swing in hitting the ball to the target.

The key to all good shot-making has to do with footwork in the golf swing. Footwork is essential in the distribution and transference of weight throughout the swing. The golfer's center of gravity is maintained, assisted, and moved back and through in hitting the golf shot from this interaction.

Balance and footwork work intimately in the timing of the swing. They are in essence the dancer leading the body to music in the dance step. They are the chief provider of rhythm and timing in the golf swing.

The following is a footwork drill that you can do for your swing.

THE FOOTWORK DRILL

Purpose: To improve the sense of footwork, balance, and timing in the golf swing.

Emphasis: In this drill the golfer takes a golf ball and begins to toss it to an object or person underhanded, say about eight to fifteen feet away. In doing so he is to toss the ball in such a way that it lands softly at the target.

The golfer is to take notice as to how he produces the motion of the throw and how his arms, hips, and feet work together in this interaction. The feet and their motion, along with the motion of the hips, release the swing of the arms and toss of the ball to its intended target on cue with the correct estimation of effort. There's a rhythm to this in which the arms and hips work together in a swinging motion. Picture the toss to a child as a good visual image on this and you'd got it.

There is a second part of this drill that you can do that goes like this: The golfer uses a golf club this time. He takes a club and places it out in front of him as if he were holding the club like it was a cane. He now works the knees and feet back and through in a simulating swing as he continues to hold the "cane" with his hands.

He now holds the club with just the left hand and allows the right hand to move back and through in motion with the knees and feet in their motion. The purpose here in this part of the drill is to teach the interaction of the necessary lower body position, what the knees, feet, and balance are doing, and have to do in good footwork in the swing.

End Result: A golfer who has developed the proper sense of footwork and balance in the golf swing.

Rhythm in the Golf Swing

There is another fundamental that is integral to the laws of movement and that has to do with the manner in which you swing the club: Rhythm. This component is the "music section" of the golf swing. Percy Boomer called "rhythm the very soul of golf."[26]

Let's examine this in more detail. Let's start with a definition so we're in agreement over terms here. The dictionary states: rhythm, noun, is any kind of movement characterized by the regular recurrence of strong and weak elements. Rhythm denotes the regular patterned flow of movement in physical activity. Good examples of this are music, dancing, singing, and writing.

Percy Boomer further stated rhythm as being "a flowing motion of timed movements..."

The Wave Principle

Nature provides an excellent example for us to emulate in the golf swing: the motion of the ocean tides. I call this in golf "The Wave Principle". The tide has a pattern that occurs with some definite regularity: it comes in after building up a strong concentrated wave and then releases the build up of energy; once released, it goes back into a weaker, more dispersed passive

26. Quote from: *On Learning Golf*, by Percy Boomer

The golf swing as a sideways toss or throw to the target

motion as gravity counteracts on the forward motion. Once again the build-up and release of this pattern repeats over and over again. In hitting a golf ball to its intended target the golfer utilizes a principle in nature similar to that of the tide in the ocean.

The golfer, in swinging the club back, effects a transfer of weight and builds up a coil of potential energy that once built-up is ready to be released like the wave in our example from nature. The forward swing to the target is the strong element in this regular patterned flow as all elements are harnessed for release at impact (like the tide going in).

This action in moving the body back and forth in a balanced manner, in an "interplay of held positions," building up the coil and then releasing it through the ball, is the "rhythm" or music section of hitting a golf shot.

Good players develop a fine sense of regularity of flow and predictable repetition of their golf swings. You have probably heard the comment "that he has a good repeating swing"—that's rhythm and balance working together, and acting as the key component in the golf swing. A dancer knows and moves to the rhythm of the beat and learns to move instinctively to the music. The competent ball striker likewise senses the rhythm of motion of the body and club back and through in unison in the golf shot.

So we have another law here in the swinging of the club and that is this:

> **ALL WELL EXECUTED GOLF SHOTS ARE THE RESULT OF A RHYTHMIC SENSE OF MOVEMENT THROUGHOUT THE SWING**

Tempo and Timing

There are two other components in the dynamics of movement that comprise a good golf swing: These are Tempo and Timing.

Tempo refers to the speed or velocity of which something is moving or swung. In the golf swing, tempo is the most individual of the components. No two golfers swing the club exactly in the same way. One player will swing the club back and through with a fast pace whereas another will swing with a much slower, deliberate speed. Likewise, certain finesse shots may require a change of pace such as the punch and knock down[27] shots or the lob shot from around the green.

Examples of fast tempos are Tom Watson, Arnold Palmer, Greg Norman, and Lanny Watkins. Exemplifying slower tempos are Julius Boros, Fuzzy Zoeller, and Nancy Lopez. There is a middle ground category of players, which there are many, who are neither fast nor slow.

The most important thing to know about tempo is keeping it controlled. Your best ball-strikers, Sam Snead, Lee Trevino and Tom Watson being good examples of this, swing the club at the same pace. Interestingly enough, the time that it takes the good player to swing the driver is almost identical for the wedge shot and the putting stroke (around 1.6 seconds)! The driver is of course swung faster than the wedge due to the bigger arc of the swing and the longer length shaft.

---

27. punch: a golf shot in which you hit down on the ball
    knock down: a golf shot in which the player hits down on the ball causing the ball to fly lower and keep from getting up in the wind

The important thing to remember here is that the tempo of the swing needs to be consistent. Swinging too fast will lead to forcing the shot and a host of errors in your shot-making. A good test in judging your swing tempo lies in the ability to feel the weight and momentum of the clubhead during the swing. Try to be more aware of this perception in your practice and playing on the course.

So we have a law about Tempo in the golf swing:

> **ALL WELL EXECUTED GOLF SHOTS ARE THE RESULT OF SWINGING IN A CONTROLLED TEMPO IN THE GOLF SWING**

TIMING is the coordination of each of the component parts of the movement of the golf swing. Its role is to regulate or control the three main components (balance, rhythm, tempo) into a synchronized, working unit. This coordination is crucial in the golf swing. Timing according to the American Heritage dictionary is a noun—the art or operation of regulating occurrence, pace, or coordination to achieve the most desirable effects, as in music, theater, athletics, or in a machine. I have worked out the following definition of TIMING in the golf swing: Timing is the perception of regulating motion and force in the interaction of positions in the golf swing. A well timed golf shot is the result of each of the basic components (balance, rhythm, tempo) of movement working together with the others.

Thus we have a law concerning this:

> **ALL WELL EXECUTED GOLF SHOTS ARE THE RESULT OF A WELL TIMED INTERCHANGE OF ITS COMPONENT PARTS IN THE GOLF SWING**

The following is a drill that the golfer can do in regards to improving his timing in his swing.

NATURAL LAWS OF GOLF TIMING DRILL

Purpose: To teach the golfer that timing involves the coordination of and regulation of balance, rhythm, and tempo in swinging the club back and through to the ball and intended target.

Golfers can drill timing in the golf swing in the following manner: Without the ball present, start by simply swinging the club back and through in a continuous fashion, observing the speed in which you can control the swing without it breaking down in balance and rhythm. The golfer just free swings the club back and through.

The golfer now works on actually hitting shots to the target, working on his timing pattern in the swing. This is done by first hitting shots say with a seven iron, making full length swings, then with half the normal pace, then with a three-quarter speed swing, and so on.

Emphasis: In this drill the stress is placed on making a series of one-piece, continuous swings in which the golfer works on combining the components of movement (balance, tempo, and rhythm) and in varying the type of shot to hit, hitting long shots and then short ones and vice versa. Some of the best players in the game vary hitting shots this way and this is an excellent way to groove in the timing pattern in the swing. Concentrate on making a series of repeating swings, in sets of five or ten, focusing on the timing and tempo that feels right to you.

The golfer can establish the right speed or swing pace by making some faster swings, then slower, and then some in between. The swing pace that's in between will most likely be the one that's right for you, one that you can control and feel you're not losing optimum clubhead speed.

End Result: A golfer who has learned to coordinate and regulate the components parts of movement and can hit well-timed golf shots to the target.

Free-swinging the club back and through without the ball helps to create the necessary sensory feel, a harmony, a blending of the body rotation and the arm swing. Many of the golfing greats have used this drill to groove-in the added feel to their swings. Sam Sneed is probably the best example of this as he is said to have swung the club 100 times or more a day to keep the feeling of a one-piece swing flowing in the swing.

The Timing Performance Triangle

Tempo, Rhythm, and Balance give us a triangle that interrelates the movement of its component parts, where we have balance at one end of this triangle, rhythm at the other, and tempo at the other corner. These three components add up to equal TIMING. So the triangle looks like this.

Timing Performance Triangle

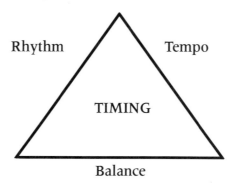

When a golfer hits a good golf shot all three of these components are working together in unison to a greater degree and actually reach a maximum level of performance (T + R + B = Timing). The successful amateur and professional golfer is "maxing out" the formula to its highest degree.

Conversely, when (one or more) of the basic components isn't working with the others and there is a breakdown in coordination, the overall result of the shot is not timed well and a poorly hit shot comes about.

I've developed a method that allows you to quickly analyze what caused a bad shot and to also know what caused a good one using the above triangle of the laws of movement in the golf swing.

If you have hit a poorly executed shot, look over which part(s) of the triangle was/were violated: was it your rhythm, balance, or was it tempo? It's not enough to say that it's your timing that was off.

Ask yourself which component was not right. For example, if you hit a pulled hook left or blocked your shot right of the target, and this led to costing you a stroke or more on that given hole, then you need to check which component of the triangle was violated. Did you lose your BALANCE? Or was it a problem of TEMPO, from swinging too fast. Was your swing too mechanical, and lacking RHYTHM?

You will find that one of these basic components will indicate as being out, and by coming to a quick conclusion on which one, you will be able, while you're walking down the fairway, to get that point in by the time you arrive at the next shot. Taking a practice swing or mentally rehearsing that particular point can be quite helpful and can remedy the situation in most cases.

You'll also find Remedies in Part II, The Mental Approach Section, that are useful for situations that have to do with the inner game of golf.

The above method can also be used to know what caused good shots that you hit. You have a feel of what's right when you hit nice shots that you can use as a feedback system. You'll find that this acts as a good reinforcer of what successfully works for you in your swing. It's also an excellent confidence booster that quickly spots what's right and strengthens your perception of what's working in your game!

Chapter VIII

Golf's Power Connection

Proper alignment is vital in the hitting of consistently good golf shots to the target. A golfer's game can stray and develop bad habits in the swing department where the alignment is faulty. The good golfer is instinctively aware of this and maintains a continuous effort to stay aligned to the ball and target and seeks the hitting position that feels ideal and right. Golfers report playing better golf when they are "in the groove" with their swings. This is due largely to their address position being correct, as well as their alignment of body and target, and of course due to their mental approach (which we'll look at in Section II on Golf's Mental Approach).

Jack Nicklaus, in his book, *Golf My Way,* stated "...that hitting specific shots, playing the ball to a certain place in a certain way, is 50% mental, 40% setup, and 10% swing.[28]

Good players set up to the ball in an athletic position that is well balanced, with the weight distributed rather evenly in the legs and feet. The lower body position in the legs and knees are springy, ready for action. The arms are supple and hang down in a relaxed position from the upper body. This set up position to the ball is often skimped on and glossed over although it is an important step.

Although this position becomes instinctive once mastered, the smart player pays strict attention to detail in the setup position, "keying" on establishing a sense of feel each time to the ball in the pre-shot routine (described later in Section II). This ensures a feeling of confidence, and heightens responsiveness for the motion of the swing to come.

The power connection in the golf swing involves the hooking up or connecting of its component parts in a one piece motion.

The golf swing works best when the body is put in an athletic position

28. *Golf My Way,* by Jack Nicklaus

of springiness, on balanced, and readied for motion. This braced connected address, as Percy Boomer and Jim Ballard refer to it, is the optimum position for the golfer to assume at set up to the ball. This positioning allows the golfer to utilize the big muscles of the upper and lower body from which the arm swing can impart power to the clubhead and ball at impact.

The braced connection

Likewise, David Leadbetter in his recent book, *The Golf Swing*, describes the building of the necessary athletic golf swing in the following manner...."The more athletic a swing you create, the more chance you have of maximizing the speed and squareness of the clubhead as it strikes the ball towards your intended target."

"To accomplish this, it is my opinion that both the direction and speed of the clubhead are controlled by your torso. Your hands and arms remain passive—think active body, passive hands." When the larger muscles of your body control the smaller muscles in your hands and arms—I liken it to the dog wagging the tail rather than the tail wagging the dog—greater consistency is the result. That is the gist of the athletic swing: correct linkage of the various components of your body with your hands, arms and club produces a dynamic motion."[29]

"The Ultimate Game of Golf" Swing is the use of this power connection in which the body is set in an athletic, readied position from which the swing can be generated and swung in a powerful way. Power in the golf swing needs to be built around this concept in order to play one's best, and is essential in hitting the ball consistently long and straight.

29. *The Golf Swing,* by David Leadbetter

Chapter IX

The Sensory Feel System—Golf's Secret in Shot-Making

In sports that involve the turning and rotation of the body with a club there is an optimum set-up position that the golfer must be in to hit consistently to the target. This is even more the case in golf as the alignment to the ball and target is vital.

The good golfer learns to work the swing and the alignment to the ball from a developed sense of feel. In other words, he's relying on a series of sensations in linking up the swing to create motion back and through to a target.

Feel emanates from a sensory perception of position—sensing where the target is and what position the body is in with respect to the club and the ball—it's the timing of the interaction of hand/eye (physical) and mind/body coordination. Feel is what brings together the physical and mental part of the game as one synchronized, working unit in the golf swing.

A sense of touch is especially crucial in the short game as such shots require more finesse and control due to variations of tempo and rhythm. Accuracy and precision are greater and are needed in the short game, to hit the approach shots as close to the flag as possible.

Percy Boomer in his book, *On Learning Golf,* describes the swing as this, "...The golf swing is a connected series of sensations or feels and when you get all these feels right and rightly connected you will swing perfectly.... Feel is sensation instead of thought, and that golf is played through the senses.... The golfer needs to learn not the technical details of a good golf shot, but the feel of it.[30]

30. *On Learning Golf,* by Percy Boomer.

The evolution of todays modern golf swing and its athletic position can be traced interestingly enough to Percy Boomer, who back in the 1940s, advocated the use of a braced connected position and the importance of feel.

Feel is the measure of sensory-motor perception of the exact amount of estimated effort required to hit or swing the club on a given shot; that's my definition for it. The target dictates the correct amount of force and feel needed on each given swing. It's up to the player "to read in" the correct estimation of effort on each given golf shot. Many a golfer tends to overlook this and gets mired down in all the technical details that absorb his attention in producing the swing.

Rule in Golf's Primary Ingredient: Feel.

Let the target dictate your swing. Be responsive to the target. This sounds rather esoteric in approach, yet all good players report that they experience something like this when they play their best. The target "communicates" the correct golf shot to hit.

Form the swing image in your mind that you want to see and create the shot that will bring about the right golf shot to hit. You're the director that reaches from the playbook of experience, pulling together the mental and physical parts of the play, shaping the action and shot in its final form before you.

Good golfers have a foundation upon which they build a sense of feel in the swing. This is an awareness of the correct feel of the body, the relaxed yet connected position at address in the golf swing, and going with a "feel key" to get the swing going to the target. This "feel key" is a form of waggle. Ben Hogan, Jack Nicklaus, Curtis Strange, and Greg Norman are good examples of this.

The whole idea of the pre-shot mental routine is to create a series of images and feelings in the form of "keys" that prepares the shot at hand for execution. These "keys" are the swing's feels that are tied to a proper sense of rhythm and timing in the golf swing. This routine will be elaborated on in more detail in Section II, of Golf's Mental Approach.

These are the laws that are tied to the principles of the golf swing that provide you with the knowledge to develop a set of fundamentals with which you can build your own "Ultimate Game of Golf" Swing!

I have broken these down into the basic principles that are powerful yet simple to understand. Along with the knowledge from the Inner Game/Mental Approach (Section II) of this book and the Strategy Game in Section III—you'll be armed with the *ultimate weapon* in your game and will be able to reach more of your true potential as a golfer.

These laws in golf are derived not only from my experience, working as an instructor and advisor to amateurs and pros, but from constant observation and research of the swings of the game's masters. They are set forth here to provide you with an understanding of golf's chief fundamentals that are not only simple to follow, but will arm your golf swing with a powerful weapon that you can use in your game.

The Outer Game

Chapter X

Outer Game of Golf Drills
For the Ultimate Game Of Golf

I've developed a series of drills for the Outer Game that will teach the fundamentals of making a powerful swing. These drills emphasize the sense of movement that is vitally necessary in making the motion of the swing; these are called the Natural Laws of Movement Drills.

These exercises are done on a gradient basis, in other words in a series of step-by-step drills building one upon the other for success.

THE INTERPLAY OF HELD POSITIONS DRILL

The first drill is the Interplay of Held Positions Drill.

Purpose: This drill is designed to create a better sense of awareness of the interplay of "held positions" that the golfer must make in the golf swing.

Emphasis: The golfer studies each of these held positions and their interplay, starting with the set-up position (Position 1). This position is a static one in which the golfer is planted at the start of the swing in an athletic position. The set-up position is very important and cannot be over-emphasized (see Drill #3 for more details). He then studies the waist-high position (Position 2) and duplicates this move, and then swings the club to the top of the backswing (Position 3). He then swings the club through to impact (Position 4), and finally swings the club through to swing's completion (Position 5).

This drill stresses the sensory feel of a continuous movement or interplay of the given positions back and forth from both sides of the swing. The drill can be worked on in slow motion, and then at a faster swing to the point where it blends into the regular swing motion.

This exercise is included here to give the golfer the overview of the necessary swing positions and is to be done to give the golfer the concept of the complete golf swing and its sense of power.

End Result: A golfer who has a better awareness of the swing's motion, its interplay of held positions, and can make a powerful golf swing.

The five positions of the golf swing

THE SET-UP POSITION DRILL

The second drill is the Set-up Position drill.

Purpose: To teach the proper set-up position to put the body in for hitting a golf shot.

The golfer stands in an erect position facing the ball with his arms first at his side with his weight evenly distributed. The emphasis of weight is on the inside and on the balls of the feet for optimum balance. The feet are shoulder-length apart opposite the ball. From this erect position the golfer bends from the waist and lower back producing a flexed, springy position with the arms now extended from his side toward the ball.

The extended arm position from the shoulders hangs slightly inward, forming the basis of a triangle with the shoulder, arms and hands. The arms however, hang down in a relaxed, not rigid position from the shoulders.

The Set-up drill

93

In this part of the drill the golfer assumes the correct posture and position without the club, paying particular attention to being on balance in a flexed, springy, readied for action position. This exercise is done several times until the golfer feels he is in the most optimum position in order to hit the ball. This will feel like a powerful, connected position that's ready for launching, where the golfer's stance and posture align as one to the ball.

In Part B of this initial exercise, the golfer assumes the above position, but now with the club in hand. He places the club directly behind the ball still standing erect, but now he lowers the club down to the ball bending from the waist and lower back. This drill can be done with your instructor or another person checking your position or with a mirror at home.

Emphasis: It's important to be positioned to the ball in this fashion so that you're not having to build-in a compensation, e.g. weight too far forward, causing a faulty foundation in your posture (spine angle). That would result in an incorrect movement, swing plane, and resultant bad habit in the swing.

End Result: A golfer who can set up to the ball correctly and is ready to make the shot to the target.

THE ALIGNMENT DRILL

Purpose: This drill teaches how to step into position, get aligned with the club to the ball and the body position to the target. You will find that all the great strikers of the ball in the game of golf utilize a pre-swing routine that incorporates a series of basic moves which they adhere to time after time.

Step One: Standing erect with the shoulders and hips, grip the club in the left or right hand, whichever you prefer. Now "walk into the shot" from the side as you look down at the target, place the club and feet directly behind the ball. Move the left foot farther apart from the right. Further adjust the feet position with the ball and target, depending on the length of the shot. Get in a comfortable position to the ball. Ideally the head, shoulders, hips, and feet are level and align to the target.

The left hand, or right if you prefer, is gripped first as you step into position with the leading foot towards the ball. Some players place both hands on the club first. Now aim the club to the target, returning your focus back to the target.

The final stance position is quickly assumed by making any necessary last adjustments for feel and comfort while keeping your shoulders, hips, and feet aligned with your body position and eyes focused on the target.

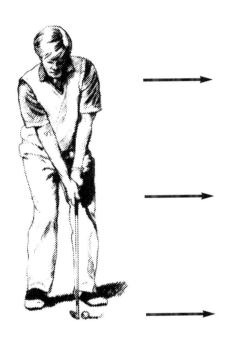

The golfer correctly aligned to the target

Emphasis: Learn to move routinely from each part of the sequence as a training pattern without having to consciously look or think about its components in the alignment process, especially the feet. Along with this "ready for action" sequence, the golfer is working towards a sense of rhythm in his set-up routine in hitting shots to the target. This drill is worked through as a routine and should be drilled as such, thereby setting the stage for the execution of the shot.

End Result: A golfer who can routinely set-up to the ball, and knows the importance of it in the golf swing.

THE TAKEAWAY DRILL

Purpose: To train the golfer to sweep the club back along the ground in a connected manner with the shoulders, arms, hips and center.

The initial move in the golf swing, the takeaway, sets the whole sequence of the swing into motion. This motion away from the ball must be "connected" or "hooked up" integrating the upper and lower body and the centering position of the spine. This is best accomplished by sweeping the club back low and in one piece movement away from the ball.

The golfer needs to drill this move away from the ball and should do so with emphasis on pushing the club back with the left shoulder, arms and hips as the weight becomes centered behind the ball. The use of a video camera or a mirror is very useful in checking the golfer's correct position in doing so.

When the backswing has reached waist high, the weight has shifted to the back leg and the club is extended holding the triangle position. The spine and head position are centered behind the ball now directly in line—the hands and wrists begin to hinge or cock automatically as the club is further rotated by the upper body (torso) and the hips and center of the body to the top of the back swing.

The takeaway must "hook up" or "feel connected" in the move away from the ball and towards the back leg. As a matter of fact, a good backswing is the key to a good shot to the target. Jack Nicklaus is an excellent example of the extended, one-piece takeaway in the golf swing.

The golfer moving the club back along the ground together with the triangle intact creating a weight shift onto the back leg

Emphasis: The takeaway should be drilled to ensure that it's correctly applied. As a checkpoint, the toe[31] of the club should be facing up at waist high in the backswing and extended into the triangle. If the club of the toe is pointed right at waist level, the club face is open; if it's left or "hooded," it's shut or in a closed position to the ball. These incorrect positions are the result of a breakdown in the takeaway position of the major component parts: head/shoulder, chest/torso, arms/hands, and hips/body center, causing an incorrect manipulation of the hands and wrists.

A) Toe up at waist-high position in the swing.
Incorrect positions: B) toe (left) closed and C) toe (right) open.

31. toe: the base or lower tip of the golf club

In doing this drill, the training stress is on maintaining the triangle and the centered position of the head and spine behind the ball. You can either use a mirror, your instructor, or a golfing buddy standing behind you to check your position by swinging the club back in the backswing to waist-high and placing the club in his hand. A good name for this drill is "Put The Club In My Hand Drill."

Putting the Club in my Hand Drill

End Result: A golfer who can make a one-piece takeaway with the shoulders, arms, hips, and center working together.

As the club passes waist level it is swung around and up to the top of the backswing to approximately ear level or slightly higher, at which point the lower body from the ground up (via the feet, legs, and hips) has already begun to reverse the flow of motion, unwinds and moves back to the ball, thus releasing the clubhead into the back of the ball.

This shifting of gears is the hallmark of the good golfer's swing versus the inexperienced one, and happens at laser-like speed in which the right side, like a piston, fires the powerful drive and thrust of the lower body platform into the ball. This releases the stored up energy potential of the backswing up against the braced left side "wall" position of the left hip, leg and foot.

It seems that there's been a lot of confusion and misconception over the years about the role of the firing of the right side in the downswing.

The release of the right side into the ball is a direct response to the coiling. It allows the release of that built-up force into the left side (held) position and ball at impact.

Remember that *power in the golf swing is based upon the interplay of held positions and alternating motions*—without such interplay there is no real delivery of power. With this interplay, there is harnessed power in the golf swing. The biomechanics of power derive from the components of its base and platform, and displacement of interplay of held positions.

Witness the golf swings of Bobby Jones, Ben Hogan, Byron Nelson, Tom Watson, Jack Nicklaus, and Sam Snead as excellent examples of this—exploding power into the ball.

DRIVING THE RIGHT SIDE IN THE GOLF SWING DRILL

Purpose: To learn to powerfully drive the right side into the shot in the golf swing.

The right side move can be worked into a drill in the following manner: At the top of the backswing, as the hands arrive at about ear level, the hips, knees, and feet act like pistons and release the coiled upper body. They unload the club shaft at the ball and into the held left side position or "wall" with the triangle and center position returned to its original position at the ball, at which point the hips now release followed by the shoulders and head as the golfer's eye follows the flight of the ball to its intended target.

Emphasis: This drill stresses the importance in developing the feeling of the right side driving towards the ball and against the left side position. Also pay attention to finding the correct pace or speed that you can swing the club without losing control.

Just as the left side sets up the initial move away from the ball at the onset of the backswing with the left heel releasing or moving back behind the ball, so does the right side initiate the forward swing to the target. The hips, legs, knees, and feet *drive* into the shot, with the hips leading, squaring up the rotation of the body, and thus allowing the lower body, arms, and hands to fire into the ball at impact position. This sequence causes a kinetic chain of release at impact to be maximized.

This whole sequence of movements is very quick: it takes only a second and a half, and the clubhead reaches speeds of over 100 miles per hour! So it's necessary to realize that one is striving to cause a swing that is as direct and continuous in its response as possible without deliberating and thinking too much about it. I think that Jones, Hagen, Nelson, Sneed, Nicklaus, Watson, and Trevino are some of the best to emulate in their one-piece swings.

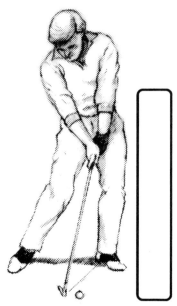

The right side driving "into the wall" and left side in the swing

Note!

These drills are listed in Summary form at the end of this section for you to refer to and use over again. Follow the sequence of the program here and drill these steps of the swing's kinetic chain until it has become second nature and you have mastered the movement as your own. The complete description of each drill is given earlier in this section. The Summary Section is for quick reference.

Summary of Outer Game Drills of
The Ultimate Game of Golf

1) THE SET-UP DRILL

Purpose: To teach the correct position to put the body and club in for hitting a golf shot.

Emphasis: Creating a springy, on balance position. Arms extending down and slightly in. The position is relaxed, the knees are slightly flexed.

End Result: A well-balanced, poised position from which to hit the ball from.

2) THE ALIGNMENT DRILL

Purpose: To develop a routine in which the golfer is comfortably set up to the target with the proper body and club position.

Emphasis: Alignment should be walked into with the right foot first and the club positioned at the same time behind the ball to the target.

End Result: The golfer optimumly aligned and readied to hit a golf shot.

3) THE TAKEAWAY DRILL

Purpose: To teach the golfer the correct takeaway movement as a one piece unit going back in the backswing.

Emphasis: Allow the left foot and side to initiate the swing. Clubhead sweeps back to waist level with the triangle position intact. Weight shifted to back leg.

End Result: A takeaway that is extended, connected, and sets the swing response in motion.

4) THE ONE PIECE TO THE TOP DRILL

Purpose: To teach the feeling and movement of the swing being swung back in one piece to the top of the swing.

Emphasis: Create a sweeping one-piece movement with the left side starting back (left shoulder, foot and knee) in the backswing.

End Result: A one-piece, completed backswing that is readied for firing to the target.

5) THE FREE SWING DRILL

Purpose: To teach the golfer how to make a one-piece swing back and through in the golf swing.

Emphasis: Work on developing a flowing interaction between the upper and lower body movement in the swing that is smooth, balanced and well timed in the swing.

End Result: A well timed, flowing, and powerful golf swing to the target.

6) FIRING THE RIGHT SIDE TO THE TARGET DRILL

Purpose: To teach the powerful move of the legs, hips, feet and right side driving towards and against the "wall" position of the left side.

Emphasis: Create a sweeping one piece movement. Allow the left foot and knee to start the swing going back to the top and then the right side initiating the driving of the forward swing into the ball.

End Result: A powerful release of the right side in hitting the ball to the target.

Chapter XI

Additional Drills For The Outer Game Section

I've included four additional swing drills: The Step Back/Step In Drill, The Swing Lever Drill, The Swing Key Drill, and The Towel Drill. They are listed in order of importance. These are excellent drills and exercises that accompany the Outer Game section swing drills. These can be used to complement and strengthen the above drills and can also be used as remedies when you get off in your swing.

STEP BACK/STEP THROUGH DRILL

Purpose: To develop the proper coordination and timing of the upper and lower body in the golf swing. An excellent drill that teaches the body the correct feeling of rotation and connection in the golf swing.

Emphasis: In this drill the golfer swings the club back and steps back in the same motion in the backswing, bringing the club to about ear level position and drives the body via its center into the shot in the forward swing to the target. The hands follow the body's lead. Balance is important here in this drill and the golfer should work on stepping into the left side position in hitting the ball and timing the firing of the held positions. The golfer finishes the swing with the weight on his left side.

End Result: A golfer who can coordinate the upper and lower movement in the golf swing in a well-timed, back and through motion.

The golfer (A) stepping back with the club at the same time on the takeaway from the ball and (B) stepping into the shot by driving the legs, hips and feet of the lower body into the ball

THE SWING LEVER DRILL

Purpose: To provide a mechanism or "lever" that smoothly activates the swing into motion.

Emphasis: Drill use of a waggle, kick of the right knee or float of the weight back and forth to activate the swing from its, start position.

End Result: A swing lever or "gear" effect that helps get the swing started from its start position into that of a proper takeaway in the backswing.

SWING KEY DRILL

Purpose: To develop a consistent, set physical motion—a "swing key"—that ties together the golf swing into an integrated movement.

Emphasis: Focus on what you do that gets the swing to work as a unit and practice it as a pattern or swing key rather than an isolated series of swing thoughts. An example of this would be say, in the takeaway, a forward press, a swing waggle, taking the club back "low and slow," and in the overall swing, "staying connected," or "putting your best swing on it."

Whatever you use, the idea is to align or centralize your swing thoughts to one swing key, and get the swing in motion without undue delay. Otherwise you run the risk of thinking too much with the swing, and getting tied up with its mechanics, which will inhibit its motion.

Practice your swing key using one of the above, or your own, with an iron or wood (the driver especially), hitting shots to a target, focusing on that specific "key concept" that gets the swing working for you. Work on making this part of your routine in your swing and in doing so you'll add consistency to your ball striking.

End Result: Use of a central thought or "swing key" that packages the mechanics of the golf swing into an integrated motion.

THE TOWEL, BEACH BALL OR BASKETBALL DRILL

Purpose: To teach the importance of linking or "hooking up" the backswing and forward swings to the target.

Emphasis: The inside of the left arm and chest are linked together or "hooked up" as a hinged unit in the swing. Use of a towel under the left or both arms will produce the feeling of the linkage of the component parts working properly. The towel will remain in place when the swing is properly executed, which is when the shoulders, arms, and center maintain the triangle position connection.

Place the towel under the left arm and start hitting three-quarter shots to the target with a seven or eight iron. Hit twenty to thirty shots this way, working up to fuller shots and clubs as you go, getting the feeling more ingrained in the swing.

Now without the towel, hit shots with a random selection of shots, short and longer ones and notice how the torso and arms work together as a unit in the swing. Concentrate on maintaining this relationship until it becomes more second nature for you.

You can also try this drill in another way by using a semi-inflated beach ball or basketball. The golfer places the ball under his arms and across his chest from which the object is to swing back and through without dropping the ball from this held interactive position.

In addition to this, the golfer, with the use of the beach-ball or basketball, can get the same swing feeling of hooking up the swing by tossing the ball sideways behind him to a person or object. The golfer will find that the ideal manner in which to pass the ball is with the legs, hips and torso working together as a unit. In this way he is moving from his center without effort and in a more powerful way than using his upper body strength.

End Result: A golfer whose upper and lower body movements link up, producing a more efficient, well-timed swing rotation to the intended target.

The golfer with a beach ball or towel under his arm or arms and held into the chest in a braced athletic position. The golfer then swings the club back and through from the center of his body with the ball or towel throughout the swing.

Section II

The
Inner Game/
Mental Approach
to Golf

SECTION II
THE INNER GAME/MENTAL APPROACH TO GOLF

The
Inner
Game

Chapter I

Golf and The Mind Game

Throughout the history of the game, the search for the "secret of golf" has been ardently pursued by its followers, each looking to solve its mystery and achieve its "ultimate state of mind." This pursuit has led to many inner circles, and to the keen insights of its legendary masters of the game and a plethora[32] of gratuitous advises from its followers. What is the clue to its mystery? Perhaps, Arnold Houltain stated it best, back in 1908 in his book, *The Mystery of Golf.*

"Ah! To think that there's an easy answer invites folly. One needs only to ask the man who thinks he has mastered the game to come forth, and to consult the multitude of driven souls who have surrendered to the whims and ways of "Old Man Par."

"The clue surrenders to a three-fold analysis: physiological, psychological, and social. In the first place, no other game has so simple an object or one requiring, apparently, so simple an exertion of muscular effort. To knock a ball into a hole — that seems the epitome of ease. It is a purely physiological matter of moving your muscles so. Yet to move the muscles in a very precise manner in the swing is the problem that faces the golfer. Without a doubt the ball must be impelled by muscular movement: how to co-ordinate that muscular movement — that is the physiological factor in the fascination of golf.

"In the second place, when the novice golfer begins to give some serious consideration to the game, he discovers that there is such a thing as style in golf, and that a good style results in good golf. He begins to think there must be some knack to playing the game, a skill that has to be learned by the head and taught by the head to the muscles. Accordingly, he takes lessons, reads instructional books, laboriously thinks out every stroke, and by degrees comes to the conclusion that the mind has as much to do with golf as the hands and eyes. It is here that the psychological factor, an *inner game* comes into play.

32. plethora: superabundance; excess. [derived from the Greek 'plethora,' fullness]

"In the third place, despite having made some progress, he discovers that the character of his opponent and the quality of that opponent's play exercise a most extraordinary influence over him. This is the social factor.

"There is no other game in which these three fundamental factors—the physical, mental, and the social—are so extraordinarily combined or so constantly called into play. Some sports, such as football, baseball, fencing, and weight lifting call chiefly for muscular activity, judgment, and nerve; others, such as chess, and card games, call upon the intellect only.

There is no other game with this combination of factors. The whole anatomical frame is brought into a physical yet delicate action at every stroke. Second, the mind plays a key part in governing the action of the muscles. Third, the character and temperament of both you and your opponent powerfully affect you. To play well, these three factors in the game must be most accurately adjusted, and their accurate adjustment is as difficult as it is fascinating."[33]

The Inner Game and its Mental Approach is the one that either makes it all happen or denies one success in golf. It's this part of golf that gives the pros the most trouble and is the make or break point in your game. Golf and how you play it is a State of Mind.

Mastering the game is possible only when all three factors are under control, and, of these, the Mental factor is the key factor.

Every golfer who has taken up the game can attest to the game's never ending challenges, frustrations, moments of mountain highs and valley lows, of despairing torments that reach far to the very depths of their golfing souls.

I have been a student of the mind game for many years now. When I left collegiate golf and school in 1972 with some wounded pride and failure of purpose, I decided to find out what thwarted and stopped me from reaching my true potential as a player. Where this would lead I didn't know. I was determined however to remedy this situation for my own personal sense of accomplishment, and get the results that I felt capable of reaching. I would like to share with you here some of the insights and advises that I have learned and found to work with good players of the game.

The mental character of this game is etched into the very fabric of golf and life itself. It is a microcosm of life which has continued to challenge, reward and dash the greatest hopes amongst even the strongest of iron-willed men and women golfers.

33. *The Mystery of Golf,* by Arnold Houltain

Surprisingly enough, little is known about the "Mental Game of Golf." Amidst hundreds of books that have been written over the last one hundred years or so on the subject of golf instruction and its swing mechanics, only a handful have been devoted to this area itself. This is interesting when you consider that the mind game is agreed to be the most important to master.

There are three books over the span of a century that stand out on the subject. They are in order of popularity, *The Inner Game of Golf* (1977), written by Tim Gallwey, *Golf In The Kingdom*, a metaphysical tale of an encounter with a wizened golf guru (1975) by Michael Murphy, and *The Mystery of Golf* (1908), written some years ago by Arnold Haultain, whose keen insight into the mind game is rather extraordinary for its time. Golfers even then were acutely aware of the importance of the mind game and how it meant either success or failure in their game.

There are many fine swingers of the game, golfers that can hit the ball with grace and authority and shoot good scores, yet only a small percentage ever really reach the top ranks as an amateur or pro and stay there. Armed with a good swing, many golfers can't take their game from the range to the first tee without it coming apart, having the wheels come off somewhere on the course, with a ruined score for that day.

Why is this? What are the phenomena that determine success and deny ability among so many players of this great game? Is golf that hard to master?

Golf's mental approach has not really been taught. You either have one, or it became your downfall and ruin in your game. Many golfers never really become top players because of it. That has been the case until now. *The Ultimate Game of Golf* book is designed to highlight key breakthroughs in all three major parts of the game of golf to make you a better golfer and a real scoring threat in your conquest of "Old Man Par."

Good players agree that the game of golf is very much mental in its approach. Jack Nicklaus, golf's premier player in the modern era and perhaps the greatest ever, stated his view in his book entitled, *Golf My Way*. "I feel that hitting specific shots, playing the ball to a certain place in a certain way, is 50% mental picture, 40% setup, and 10% swing".[34]

Many golfers feel it's 75%, some even say as much as 90% mental. Surveys that my staff and I have done with golfers at all levels, especially players in single-digit handicaps confirm this. In fact as the player becomes better, his fascination with it and appreciation for it increase in his game.

34. *Golf My Way*, by Jack Nicklaus

Many a golf tournament is won, not by a barrage of birdies and eagles down the final nine holes, but by the player who makes the least amount of mistakes, can stay in control and manage his game well, because he has the best mental attitude.

The purpose of this section of the book is to introduce you to the natural laws and their principles that have been discovered concerning the Inner Game and its Mental Approach, and the self management that is needed to master golf. It's based on actual key principles that have been found to work successfully for all good players that also can work for you in your game.

This is probably the most overlooked and neglected part of your game of golf. This aspect of the game is not taught in golf instruction even today, where 90–95 percent of the emphasis is on the swing and its mechanics. Yet the trend is moving towards the mental part as more and more Tour and good players seek out mental coaches in their games.

The swing is also a vital part of the game to develop. Both parts depend on each other, yet it's the ability to think smart, concentrate, and control the action in a confident state of mind that produces winning results on the course when the pressure is on and you need to perform.

It's rather ironic that so much attention has been centered on swing mechanics and the pursuit of the "perfect golf swing," yet those who excel at golf are those who, besides having good sound swings, have developed mental approaches that enhance their chances to consistently outperform the rest of the competition.

As a matter of fact, you will most likely see the same names each year in the top twenty on tour over a stretch of two to three years winning eighty percent of all the golf tournaments and prize money, leaving the rest of the field behind in state of bewilderment; these players undoubtedly perform at a higher level and state of mind than the rest, and they're playing against the world's best!

Most golfers want to play their best and work to varying degrees to do so; yet the majority find themselves unable to do so for a number of reasons, be it their lack of discipline or motivation, their career, job, or family demands.

Golfers on the whole feel they are capable of playing as much as fifty percent better, and do at times, especially if they are getting the right instruction on the swing, and in their course management[35] and strategy.[36] They would find the time to practice and play more if they could see this potential coming to fruition in the form of lower scores and increasingly better results. A good round of golf is a real morale booster, and to play consistently at or below your handicap is a rewarding experience. Each chapter has a drill or series of drills to apply to this part of your game so that you get the most out of the materials. The drills are for the golfer's use and application to his own game.

I can guarantee that you will play better, smarter, more confident golf than you have before, as you follow "The Ultimate Game of Golf" Program in this book and apply it to your game.

This book, *The Ultimate Game of Golf,* represents that journey on an unmapped road, for all the golfers who have felt that they haven't reached their true potential and feel deep down that they would if they could just cast aside the negative doubts, fears and lack of self confidence.

Why is it that among golfers with equal physical ability, some are winners while others are losers? Why are ordinary players with certain handicaps still winners? What are they doing on a more consistent basis in their thinking than the rest of us?

Why is it that your best golfing friend or business associate beats you consistently, being equally matched in handicap, in competition and those friendly bets between you, but not during a casual game of golf out on the "old links"? It's because that player has a better mental approach and rises to the occasion, despite the contrary.

Golf is not just a game, it's a composite of two games in one: the Outer Game, the physical act of striking the ball and the Inner Game; one's thoughts and creative process.

There is also a third game, the Scoring/Strategy Game that is quite important because it's the scoring department that produces the results of the other two (see Section III), but for our purposes here the Strategy game is an extension and by-product of the mental aspects and it's process of where to hit the ball.

Although no two golf swings you make are the same, the swing is (or should be) an instinctive response to your intention and thought process wherein you make the correct swing to a given target based on the right amount of feel to hit that particular shot or putt.

35. course management: the state or condition of administering one's mental and scoring games in golf
36. strategy: a plan of action that the golfer executes in the scoring game

Chapter II

The Mental Aspects
of Golf

Golf is a game that involves hundreds or more mental calculations during an eighteen hole round, and where one lacks a true knowledge of the mind, to that degree one is not in control or fully causative.[37] It is a game played against a formidable opponent, "Old Man Par," who like his friend the sea, works in a variety of seemingly cruel and mysterious ways, lying in wait to wreak havoc and dash the hopes of the best of players. The real opponent, however lies not so much with "Old Man Par," but with a region of man not fully known, a territory that remains the last frontier to man and all golfers, "a terra incognita," known as the human mind.[38] The mind either works for you, overcomes barriers and obstacles with analytical solutions for success or it operates on incorrect, reactive information and works against you.

Golfers do not play up to their true potential because they are adversely affected by their own minds—unwanted emotions, upsetting memories, losses, and self doubts. It's this area that holds the golfer back from playing his best. This reactive part of the mind not only inhibits and interferes with a positive state of mind, but is the barrier to an individual's control. It's responsible for keeping the golfer from achieving any consistent performance. I'm sure that you have wondered why even the best players aren't able to perform at the highest level of their ability on a consistent basis. It's because of this phenomenon.

Although there had been some advance over the recent years in the direction of a mental approach for golfers such as *Golf in the Kingdom,* by

37. causative: effective, able to get results
38. mind: the purpose of the mind is to resolve problems relating to survival and to direct the effort of the organism according to these solutions (*Scientology 0–8*)

Michael Murphy, and most notedly the book, *Inner Game of Golf,* by Tim Gallwey—I still considered that there existed an important *missing link* in the game which hadn't been found that holds together its foundation and essence. This would either pave the way for success or open the door to failure in my endeavor as a player and as an advisor to golfers.

Golf's missing link: The Mind

The Inner Game of Golf, by Gallwey got people thinking less about their swings and more about the mental game of golf. Gallwey found that golfers spent too much time dwelling on the negative part of their game, being critical of themselves, and that many of them reinforced their failures through a system of negative, inner dialogues that prevented them from playing their best.

He offered a way to sidetrack the negative, bad experience and focus the golfer's attention more on hitting the ball with a simple but workable "back and hit" remedy in their shot-making. It's a known fact that golfers spend too much time thinking about hitting the ball rather than doing it!

Golfers for some time now have been frustrated and puzzled by this part of the game and have realized its importance in the playing of golf. Arnold Haultain's book, *The Mystery of Golf,* written back in 1908, portrays the enigmatic character of the game and attests to its surprising difficulty.

It was during the summer of 1976 that I stumbled upon two breakthroughs that would later produce together a workable mental approach in golf. These were 1) the development of a mental approach program for golfers and 2) a new awareness and advancement in my own game.

There is a close cause and effect relationship between the mind and body. The mind formulates solutions and decision points based on the information provided it and the body carries out those actions in motion and movements.

This relationship is affected by the player's current state of mind. The player's mental state is influenced by his emotions, which play an important part in his decision and shot-making process. Negative, unwanted emotions can wreck a golfer's performance. Thus what one pictures and perceives can affect the quality and outcome of the golf shot.

Golf is not the easiest of games to play. Besides a sound swing, the golfer needs to have a mental edge in order to master the game. All good golfers realize this, and work on developing one in order to master the game. One chief problem that golfers have with the game stems however from a lack of consistency between these two systems (mind and body), and it's this breakdown of coordination between the two that inhibits the golfer's ability to perform.

The interplay of these systems is vital and necessary in its communication and feedback, yet is subject to breakdown due to a chief factor—the reactive part of the mind, which is the source of its inconsistency and error. We will be examining this in more detail in this section.

Chapter III

Golf's Real Opponent: The Mind

An interesting fact that I noticed with many golfers was that their games on the golf range differed from their play on the course. This difference ranged as much as a swing of five to ten strokes. Once the golfer crossed from the practice range to the "front lines" of the first tee of the course, he became affected by a combination of areas in both his physical and mental game, such as faulty mechanics in the swing, lack of ability and confidence in hitting certain shots, frustration too difficult to handle, and loss of mental control of his emotions. These factors add more complexity to the game and take the player's attention away from hitting the ball where it should go.

Making the swing becomes more stressful, and these efforts pervade other areas of the game, thus preventing a sense of balance between the mental thought process and the physical interaction of hitting golf shots. This pattern inhibits the player's confidence and ability to perform. Golf is played at its best when it is kept simple in approach.

There was a significant difference in most golfers' games when it came to playing on the course for a real score. Many golfers at the amateur and pro level with great looking swings and a scratch handicap at the range, can't shoot eighty or better on a consistent basis under the pressure of competition.

Another surprising observation was the phenomenon of golfers who, with lesser physical skills, were able to get more out of, and out perform more skillful players on a consistent basis. They seemed to have a less complex system of doing it and maximized their potential with better mental approachs than their opponents.

This inability to play up to one's potential was the single reason that golfers experienced intense frustration or burnout in their game. It was this area that intrigued me the most, both personally and in the observation of other golfing students' and players' games.

My research into why this was the case with golfers narrowed the problem down to two main areas: 1) false information about the golf swing and the teaching of the game, and 2) the golfer's changing and inconsistent mental state of mind.

Golfers at the top in both the amateur and pro ranks excel at each of these areas where they have learned to apply what works in their game, stick to fundamentals and have a workable mental approach in which they stay in control under pressure.

Chapter IV

Golf's Missing Link

As stated before golfers do not play up to their potential because they are limited by their own minds—it's the unwanted emotions, upsetting memories, losses, and lingering self doubts that block the path to better golf. It is this phenomenon that holds the person back from playing to his true potential. Up until now, there has been no real way to get rid of the accumulation of past unpleasant experience in life for the player, to play unburdened from such obstacles.

The first requisite for improving one's mental performance lies in gaining a better understanding of your mind, its fundamentals and how it works. Golf's mental approach has been rather limited in its development and golfers have been playing golf for some time without an instruction manual of how their minds work for them and this can thwart the best of intentions and performance.

When you're about to close out your opponent or shoot your best score ever and you hit it out of bounds on an easy shot to the green, then something is wrong and that something is playing havoc to your success. This is what has been the problem and the missing link to maintaining a consistent state of mind performance for the golfer. How to handle this is what this book is all about.

For many years I have studied numerous works in the field of psychology, Eastern philosophies, and the humanities. Over the years, I have applied these works to sports enhancement, particularly to golf, in the development of a mental approach. From this study, I found that there were some truths— yet these works lacked a true understanding of the mind. What was lacking in this field was a science of the mind that could systematically, predictably improve an individual's mental performance. The performance of an athlete has all to do with mental performance.

I have chosen an American work, an actual best-seller that from the results I have seen works best. It has been used by professional and Olympic athletes. It's a most definitive work, "a manual for the human mind," that imparts a knowledge of the mind, how it works and how it can be tapped for more success potential for the golfer and any athlete. This is the self-improvement book, *Dianetics, The Modern Science of Mental Health,* by L. Ron Hubbard.

Just as I have tried to provide you with information concerning breakthroughs made in the game of golf, I have provided insights and valuable viewpoints in this work from several other sources in the Outer Game and Scoring Game Sections.

In the research that I have done on the Inner Game and its Mental Approach, *Dianetics* reveals the most effective data to date concerning the role of the mind, its fundamentals and how it can work for you (or against you).

L. Ron Hubbard discovered that the mind essentially was composed of mental image pictures that a person recorded in minute detail of past experience that happened to him during his life.

How The Mind Works

As described in *Dianetics,* the mind can be subdivided into two parts: the analytical and reactive mind.

The analytical mind is "the conscious aware mind which thinks, observes data, remembers it, and resolves problems." It operates like a computer and will always give a person the best answer and solution to a problem or situation, based on the data available to the person.

The reactive mind[39] is that "portion of a person's mind which works on a totally stimulus-response basis, which is not under his volitional control and which exerts force and power of command over his awareness, purposes, thoughts, body and actions."

The reactive mind works below the person's awareness level. It records all the bad experiences that have happened to the individual, the pains, fears, losses and emotional upsets. When it is doing this the analytical mind is not working and being aware of what's going on. So the individual does not have pictures of this to analyze with.

39. reactive mind: definition taken from *Dianetics and Scientology Technical Dictionary*

This part of the mind stores up all the bad things that have happened to the individual and throws them back at the person in moments of danger or upset and so dictates his actions along lines that he hasn't decided.

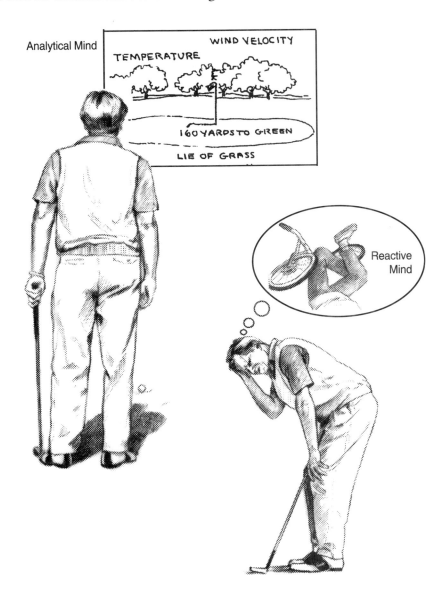

The two parts of the mind: the analytical and reactive mind

Let's take an example of a golfer who is playing along on the course in his Club Championship and is having a good tournament, playing below his handicap, and finds himself leading the final round by two strokes.

He makes a good par at the par three thirteen with a left to right six footer and feels confident and in control. Just five holes remain, and he figures an even par finish on his part will bring him victory. After a delay of what seems to have been an hour or more at the fourteenth tee, the long treacherous four hundred forty-four yard par four, the wind picks up in intensity with a threat of possible rain to the east.

He knows the importance of a good drive here. Loosening up with full swings, it's his time to hit; yet he backs off the shot however, and is indecisive[40] about going with the driver after all. A feeling of tightness grips his stomach and legs. He backs off the shot again seemingly annoyed due to the dark gathering clouds and wind and his dispersed concentration.

He hooks his drive left in deep rough towards "O.B." (out of bounds), his ball ends up close to a tree but in bounds, yet requiring a restricted backswing with no real thought of reaching the green in two. He moves the ball, however to his sudden dismay, no more than sixty yards! He finds himself in a rage and uncontrollable hurried pace, very annoyed at himself for "being such an idiot for blowing it." He rushes the next shot pulling it left of the green in tall grass green-side.

He's now upset to the "max," wanting to lash out and break something—he misses the five footer and in a blur of emotion, backhands the ball which misses the cup. He has to settle now not just for bogey but a triple bogey seven! He's beside himself. An inner rage seeks to explode inside…. His nearest opponent "snakes" in a ten-footer for par. He's lost the two stroke lead and now is a stroke behind.

He struggles to regain his composure, to fight on and overcome this sudden catastrophe, get the wheels back on and fast before it's too late. Hitting on the fifteenth hole, a relatively easy three hundred seventy-eight yard hole, he hits it left again in the rough and makes bogey five.

A threatening build up of rain clouds and shift of wind causes undue irritation. He doesn't have it, he's not really being there. He plays the last two remaining holes in a stunned, immobilized silence accompanied by a feeling of despair and hopelessness.

His body feels drained of all energy and is accompanied by an anxious

40. indecision: being uncertain; doubtful; not carrying through one's intention

nervous feeling. Crushed, he walks away once again in disgrace, "it's hopeless after all" (he says to himself), "I lost again, another close one that I let slip away," "I can't play this game of golf no matter what," "I'm a loser" — is the internal negative, dialogue of the present moment for this golfer.

What happened to this golfer has undoubtedly occurred to you in similar fashion as well, not just once but most likely a number of times—and how many times will this scene repeat itself in your game causing the frustration and inner torment of the mind? Let's examine here why such mental phenomena occur and how they can adversely affect a golfer's performance.

In the above example all was going well with our golfer who had forged ahead with a two stroke lead over his nearest competitors, with just nine holes remaining in the club championship. If we roll back the action, our golfer's misfortunes started right around the fourteenth, the course's most difficult hole, where the last remaining groups in the tournament were bunching up in the presence of rain clouds and winds from the east, for the final confrontation over the last holes.

There was a change in our golfer's mood and mental attitude that was concurrent with the shift to more adverse weather conditions of the moment: our golfer became more irritable and tempermental and lost control of his game at this point, losing not only his two stroke lead due to a series of bad, miscalculated shots, but lost his cool and composure and was out of the running, a mess of nerves, irritation and stress at his misfortune.

Our golfer finds that he has a problem or pattern of events that goes completely sour, against his intentions, when things are going "right", and that he doesn't know why. He finds such a situation just doesn't happen once but is a series of unpleasant experiences that have piled up in his life, that undermine his self-confidence. How many people achieve winning their club championship after all?

If our golfer knew his mind better and was aware of the influence of the *reactive* mind, he would know that such incidents of past painful experiences, upsetting memories, caused him to react unknowingly without being able to control his actions; in this case stemming from his experiences not just as a golfer but in other areas of life (not just sports).

Adverse weather conditions having to do with heavy rain and wind, thunder and lightning would act as an extreme irritant and restimulator, causing our golfer to get nervous, lose control, concentration and confidence while under the influence of the reactive mind. According to *Dianetics,* "a restimulator is an approximation of the reactive mind's content or some part thereof continually perceived in the environment of the organism."[41]

Becoming separated as a youngster from one's parents and lost in a crowd of people at the county fair can act as a restimulator in later life, when one attends a professional baseball game and "one feels lost," can't find one's way back to his seat in the grand-stands, and now suddenly feels extremely scared, uneasy and disoriented to his surroundings. Other such examples of restimulators would have to do with noises, voices, crowds, spaces, and objects that one feels affected by.

When similar stressful conditions approximate those of a past painful experience (emotional pain, upsetting loss) that have been recorded in the reactive mind, the individual experiences to a greater or lesser degree those same feelings.

In our example, this golfer had experienced a bad incident when he was quite young, at age eight when he and his older brother were riding their bicycle through an open field just beyond that of the park. What had happened at that time was a storm front suddenly began raining hard and there was lightning and thunder happening all of a sudden. His brother in an effort to hurry them on, yelled, "you need to go faster as you'll never make it home in time." This caused him along with the crack of lightning around him to pedal faster and he lost control and fell off his bike onto the ground, injuring his arm and shoulder.

This incident formed the earliest on a chain of related similar incidents that would later happen to him under "stressful" conditions that would affect his performance in other life situations, sports and his golf. Such incidents can become and do get "keyed in."[42]

One of such related incidents was the time in his sophomore year in high school when in a crucial, regional football game with the team up by a touchdown, with under one minute left in the game, our golfer/football player had a key opportunity to put the game away as he had beat his opponent and was wide open downfield with the quarterback about to throw a long "bomb" his way. All week despite strenuous daily workouts, spirits and stress ran high in preparation for the big game and our football player

41. restimulator: definition taken from *The Dynamics of Life* by L. Ron Hubbard
42. keyed in: a moment when the environment...is itself similar to the dormant engram. At that moment the engram became active. It is "keyed in," and can thereafter be dramatized or restimulated in the person's present time environment. Each person accumulates these incidents in life and has chronic problems with stress from these areas.

was keyed up and didn't get much sleep.

As he continued to run in stride with the long toss on its way, the home team crowd sensed him being all open on the field and victory at hand, let out a thunderous roar in response to the beckoning cheerleaders—the crowd assembled in the stands kicked and stomped their feet wildly causing a momentary, rumbling sound "like" thunder in the background.

As he drew the ball into him amidst the clamor of the crowd and opposing players now close in pursuit of him, an undue tenseness and tightness in an instance gripped his stomach and legs... he dropped the pass, the ball veering off to the left of his arms and shoulders, and was picked off by one of the opposite team secondaries, who ran the interception back close enough from where they went on to score and converted their extra point to two and beat the home team by a single point, to everyone's dismay and disappointment.

The different incidents that a person had when he got "controlled by parents and teachers," so for him, "control" is a bad thing so that he can't really control his shots—so when he makes one mistake, he "loses it," gets nervous, and frantic, etc..

It could be that another area of his life (wife, kids, work) has him worried, or he got told one too many times, "you're irresponsible," or "you get distracted too easily," in some unpleasant incident (like at school or at home), and when his boss says that "he must concentrate" more on the job at work, that can act as a restimulator.

A golfer over many years and rounds of play, especially with competition, accumulates a series of unpleasant experiences (not only from golf but in all areas of life) that creates stress for the individual. He may have at any one time a number of these stresses adversely affecting himself that get in the way of his performance.

One can think of their own examples here like the one above in which he felt the negative effects of the mind holding him back from doing the best he can in golf. I think that all of us at one time or the other have four putted or knocked a crucial drive out of bounds and lost the hole and match because of it. I can think of a few myself....

In order to play your best as a golfer, you need to be a better student of the mind. For the answers to the mind, I recommend for further reading, *Dianetics: The Modern Science of Mental Health.*

Chapter V

It's All in the State of Mind

There are many golfers, more than you can imagine, who have the necessary physical game, and can make the right shots, yet cannot perform their best on the mental side of the game—they never reach their true success potentials due to these factors described in the previous chapter.

It is these such areas of difficulty that hold back each player's ability to excel and be the best he can be at golf. There is a lot to know about the inner workings of the mind and how to control them and be on top of things.

All such mental difficulties in one's golf game such as "choking," fear of losing, anxiety, back off, shanking,[43] being unable to concentrate, having a chronic bad attitude, and a host of others are the direct result of the reactive mind's influence that causes stress and strain, breaking down concentration and inhibiting one's confidence and ability to make the right shot at the right time.

If golfers and people in general knew what held them back and stopped them from achieving their goals and objectives in golf and life—they wouldn't have that particular problem because they could "see" what it was and solve it.

You have probably heard it said that man uses only about ten percent of his true mental state in life. Imagine what things would be like in your golf and other areas if you could remove such blocks from your full natural intelligence and ability. What would things be like if your mental state was forty percent higher or more?

---

43. shanking: a golf shot veering to the right resulting from hitting the ball in the neck or hosel of the club

Each of us is born equipped with a mental computer with "built in" software programs that have far more potential and sophistication than the most advanced computers in the world today. However, we are not trained in how to use this incredible computer and its software to solve our problems and worries and unblock our full natural capacity. Unfortunately we were not given an instructional manual for the human mind to operate with.

Many a fine player fails to overcome his own "stuff" and become the best he can be because of the mind game. Many thought that legendary golfer Bobby Jones', (winner of Golf's Grand Slam[44]), greatest triumph was the gaining control over his dreaded temper which he learned to do when he had to.

It was thought by many golfers that two modern players, who possessed two of the finest swings in golf, Tommy Bolt and Tom Weiskoft, could have won far more major tournaments if they had mastered temperament and self control.

Those who win at their golf are those who believe in themselves and in their ability. They work hard at their game. Yet despite the setbacks and disappointments, they persist through the ups and downs, hang in there and maintain a mental attitude that golf is a game of integrity, sportsmanship and spirit of play that gives them the opportunity to use their God-given creative talent and skills to their fullest.

To quote an author whose name is not known but most likely a golfer at heart:

ALL IN THE STATE OF MIND

> If you'd like to win but think you can't
> It's almost a cinch that you won't.
> If you think you'll lose—you've lost
> For out in the world you find,
> Success begins with a fellow's will,
> It's all in the State of Mind.
> Many a race is lost
> Ever before a step is taken;

---

44. Grand Slam: golf's four major tournaments

And many a coward fails
Ever before his work's begun.
Think big and your deeds will grow,
Think small and you'll fall behind.
Think that you can and you will
It's all in the State of Mind.
If you think you're outclassed you are;
You've got to think high to rise;
You've got to be sure of yourself before
You can ever win a prize.
Life's battles don't always go
To the stronger or fastest man;
But sooner or later—the man who wins
Is the fellow who thinks he can.

Now that you're gaining a better understanding of the mind and are aware of a few areas that have been holding you back in golf (and in life), let's shift gears here and put things in overdrive towards the direction of you having an "Ultimate Game of Golf" and being the best golfer that you can be. All right!

Where the golfer is currently at and where he envisions being.

The first necessary step for you to make that significant improvement in your game is to take you from what we'll call Point A to Point B: Point A is a description of where you are currently—the existing scene, and Point B is where you want to be—the ideal point in which you envision success.

This could be something like: "I'm currently an eight to ten handicap player who can break 80 a couple of times out of ten, who usually wins his flight of the club championship—yet sees himself playing in the top amateur events throughout the US as a ranked player and would love to make the Walker Cup[45] team." Or something like: "I've only been playing the game for three years and am a twenty handicap but feel with hard work I could be a scratch golfer someday and win the Club Championship at my golf club."

Golfer's Self Evaluation Test.

The following is a self-test to evaluate your mental approach that I have developed to give you an idea of what condition your game is in at this stage. Total up your score and find the range of performance that you're currently at based on the last six times or more that you have played a round of golf.

Rate yourself on the following questions on a scale of 1 to 10 in regards to your mental approach in your game (in other words, how well you use these points in your game). Mark down next to the entry, or on paper, 8–10 for very good, 5–7 for good and 1–4 for poor.

Spend as much time as you need on going over these points but don't get bogged down on an answer. Just put down what you feel is correct enough on each point in question and then total up your score.

Here's the list of questions for you to answer. Rate yourself on the following areas in your golf game:

_____ 1) Concentration.
_____ 2) Accomplishing your goals.
_____ 3) Certainty in shot-making.
_____ 4) Attitude.

45. Walker Cup: amateur golf competition between U.S. and Great Britain

134

_____ 5) Confidence.

_____ 6) Handling pressure situations.

_____ 7) Controlling your shots.

_____ 8) Efficiency in strategy.

_____ 9) Use of intention.

_____10) Enjoying your game.

_____11) Good competitor.

_____12) Performing to your abilities.

_____13) Understanding of the mental approach.

_____14) Handling of upset and emotion in your game.

_____15) Consistency.

_____16) Setting of goals and targets.

_____17) Demand for improvement in your game.

_____18) Learning from your mistakes.

_____19) Knowing what caused a good shot.

_____20) Mental toughness.

Now let's see how well you did on this.

Score:	
160–200	Very Good
120–160	Good
80–120	Fair
40–80	Poor
0–40	You should take up Checkers or Badminton

Your score is an indication of how well you're doing overall in the mental approach department of your game and where you need work to improve your Inner Game Approach. Look over the questions you scored well on and the ones that you didn't do so well on.

Golfer's Self Evaluation Test— Part II

Let's take the second part of the test.

Write out a brief answer to these questions concerning your performance in golf:

1) Do you take defeat in your golf game hard?
2) Are you sometimes overly critical of your game or of a part of it?
3) Do you "blow your top" more than you should?
4) Do you have negative thoughts or impulses that affect your concentration in golf?
5) Do you find that you rush a key shot when the pressure is on?
6) After hitting poorly do you find that you speed-up your thinking process?
7) Do you often make thoughtless mistakes?
8) Does a bad shot bother you?
9) Does your mind wander while you are over the ball?
10) Are you critical of yourself in your game?
11) Do you often feel unmotivated, burned out in your golf?
12) Have you not been able to achieve the goal you've had in your game?
13) Do you consider that you are a winner at golf?
14) Do you consider that you're successful in life?
15) Do you ever get a single negative thought which hangs you up in playing golf?
16) Do you feel you haven't reached your true potential as a player yet?
17) Do you feel that you are up against a barrier or obstacle that you don't understand in your golf?
18) Are you currently stuck at a level in your game and can't seem to reach the next one?
19) Do you think that you can make a significant improvement in thinking better and smarter in your mental game?

That's the end of the test.

Now, on your answers to the questions on the second part, look these over for awhile and really take a close look at your answers. Pay particular attention to evaluating what areas you didn't score well on and are holding you back.

Look at both sections of the test and look at the areas that you're strong in and those that you're especially weak in. Are you achieving your goals in golf?

If so, great, but if you're not, then let's evaluate as objectively as possible which key areas of the game you need the most work on: Outer Game? Inner Game? The Strategy Game? All three areas or a combination of these?

Narrow down the specific individual areas from the golf test that need the most attention. From your own evaluation, formulate some kind of plan of action to improve these areas. It's best for the majority of us to have our instructor or club pro go over this with us. From this you can both get started on a definite realistic plan for improvement in your game.

The Inner Game

Practicing those particular areas on a consistent basis as determined by your plan along with the watchful eye and advice of your instructor will pay handsome dividends and a significantly improved game of golf.

It's important to point out that many a golfer is thoroughly convinced that he can't really make a big improvement in his game and has settled into "this is the way things are" mental attitude—that any real workable plan along with new breakthroughs in mental technology sounds good, yet isn't going to work for his game regardless.

All of us as golfers experience this attitude at various times—outright frustration, burnout and a sense of failure of purpose and goals. This can get so bad at times that having to hit a specific type of shot or just having to play golf at all causes more than just a mere quiver or cringe but starts a mental reaction so strong and laced with self-defeat and negative vibes that you'd think that the guy had just been sentenced or something.

Burnout and Seriousness in Golf

Burnout in one's game (and in life) is a phenomenon that occurs frequently over a period of time in a player's mental outlook, when one is not achieving one's goals and sense of purpose. This feeling has certain ways of showing itself—be it a low emotional tone[46] (such as anger, despair or apathy), physical tiredness, irritability, disrupted sleep, a general carelessness and lack of concentration in one's pre-shot mental routines and shot-making in

---

46. tone: emotional level on the Tone Scale. Tone Scale: a scale which shows the emotional tones of a person. These, ranged from the highest to the lowest are, in part; serenity, enthusiasm (as we proceed downward), conservatism, bordom, antagonism, anger, covert hostility, fear, grief, apathy

his practice, tournament play and in life in general. Burnout is a manifestation of thwarted goals and objectives. Failing to win the club championship and having finished second four years in a row when you're the best (and you know it) at your club is an example of this.

Getting too serious and bent-out of shape are two close cousins of burnout in your game. A golfer's goal becomes thwarted in his efforts to master the game and these repeated failures become a barrier or stop. There is a natural law having to do with this which explains this phenomenon. It was discovered by the author of *Dianetics,* L. Ron Hubbard, in his additional research and work contained in the Hubbard® Management Series.

> STOPS ALL OCCUR BECAUSE OF FAILED PURPOSES.
> BEHIND EVERY STOP THERE IS A FAILED PURPOSE.
> THERE IS A LAW ABOUT THIS—ALL YOU HAVE TO DO TO RESTORE
> LIFE AND ACTION IS TO REKINDLE
> THE FAILED PURPOSE. THE STOPS WILL AT ONCE VANISH.

Golfers can get revitalized in their game from the use of this principle by shifting their attention away from what's been stopping them and by focusing more on the purpose itself. Success begins with a person's will and continues forth with the intention that one can, never agreeing with the stops that occur along the way.

This is rather important to realize that any goal-setting that is to be done will be thwarted and stalled if there are barriers that you believe in and agree with.

The golfer who is stopped in his game and
has a failed purpose in golf

The golfer who is revitalized

The Importance of Goal Setting

Speaking of setting goals, set goals that are high. YOU HAVE TO THINK BIG. The size and scope of your goals is totally dependent upon what you consider you want to have happen: be it winning the Club Championship or the U.S. Open. Golfing great Bobby Jones in 1930, conceived of actually winning the Grand Slam of Golf the winter before; an unheard-of idea then, that would have bordered on blasphemy to those in the inner circle of golf at that time.

Golfer "thinking big" in his goals

Chapter VI

A Word about Emotion

Golf is a game of many emotions. Some of these emotions are beneficial and pump up the player, while others act to harm the golfer's performance. In no other sport does the player individually experience the ups and downs, the joys and frustrations harder than in the game of golf. Many a golfer has at one time or another given up the game because of its frustration and pressure.

Emotion is no more than a response to a subject, action, or an activity that evokes a particular feeling. It's derived from the French word, 'emotion,' to excite and from the Latin, 'enmo vere,' to stir up.

A golfer's feelings vary during the course of a round of golf: he hits some good shots over the first several holes and feels great, than blows his cool over the next four or five holes over a series of bad drives and putts. He then finds himself playing the remaining holes in a mental fog and haze going through the motions of just hitting the ball with no real purpose in mind, engulfed in the emotions of anger, frustration, grief and apathy.

His emotional state becomes either a hindrance or a rallying motive for him, a question of utilization: Can the golfer make these feelings work for him or are these emotions going to continue to affect him? How long the golfer sits in these emotional feelings over the course of the round and afterwards has a lot to do with the outcome of a good or bad performance.

Golf by its very nature is mercurial. Just as conditions in the game are subject to change quickly on the course so does the player's state of mind and his emotional response as he plays each hole. His mental state hangs in a precarious balance of circumstance and factors that can reverse themselves rapidly due to his shot-making and his expectations.

Most players that I have seen have a definite pattern that they go through and especially in competition, experience intense feelings, both

141

good and bad in relation to what happens. They can be up emotionally at one time, rather pleased with their shot making and then find themselves down the next after hitting a bad shot, all in one hole!

Some players tend to start slow, being a little nervous. They usually need several holes under their belts before they can open up more. Others are overly anxious to get started and come out firing for the pin and target. People react differently to pressure and stress.

Regardless of which pattern you fall into, when it comes to playing in competition and the pressure is on, the idea is to stick to that which you know you can do. Many of the pros try to maintain an even emotional level while playing as a mental strategy, in an effort to balance the highs and the lows of competition where the stakes are so high. It really becomes a question of knowing yourself, and how you respond to situations in golf that you can make work for you and not against you. This is where experience in playing in competition lends an advantage to the player who has been there and knows what to expect.

Chapter VII

Thinking Big with Your Goals

Work out here what your major goal or objective is—what you want to accomplish in the long run. Then sketch out your short and mid-range goals with a time frame period in which you're going to accomplish these.

The key to any successful goal setting in your golf has to do with making realistic goals that you can do in a confrontable series of steps that you can achieve.

I recommend that you name your overall goal, what it is that you want to achieve, and from that make a plan of what you need to do to reach that goal. Your plan should state the steps that need to happen and map out how, and what, and when you're going to do this.

I've included here an example of a successful plan that one professional golfer that I worked with used in his game. His overall goal was to be in the top thirty each year in the standings, make $350,000 to $450,000, eight top-ten finishes each year, including winning an event a year. Definitely within his potential to achieve.

His plan for each year would be, with some modifications: Improve his game in the off season on those areas that statistically were down or "not up to par" by intensive practice.

This player was a good putter averaging 30.2 putts per round but upon analysis of the top players on last year's tour who averaged 28.2 per round, he was giving up on the average two strokes every round with the putter in the scoring game, which is a seven to eight strokes total over a four round tournament!

We also discovered that his play with the longer irons was quite off his average and that of the tour leaders in hitting greens, leaving longer approach putts and bogeys on long par threes where a two or three iron was failing in its approach.

A further analysis revealed that this player started out better on front nine performances but would falter on the back nine finishes. We found this was due to stress and mental fatigue factors affecting this player. This had a link to his physical problem with his back, which would tighten up, and lapses in concentration at the wrong time.

Included in his off season "golf performance evaluation" was a program: (1) recondition and strengthen the golfing muscles in his lower back and to have him keep in a daily stretching regimen to create more flexibility to stabilize his swing; (2) identify areas of stress on and off the course that he was being affected by; (3) improve his putting with emphasis on feel in the stroke.

During the season this pro's routine went something like this: To arrive on Mondays two days before playing in the usual Pro-Am event that Wednesday, get a look at the course, play a practice round to get familiar with the layout, note key aspects about the course, especially with emphasis on the type of shots required, where trouble lay and of course getting a feel for the greens.

Tuesday's program after getting a good night's rest from all the travel and change of venue would be more intensive: Stretching and warmup exercises, getting out on the course early with his caddy to play another practice round, lunch, work on short game in the afternoon, wedge play and chipping practice, stretching exercise for his back, and a half an hour to forty-five minutes devoted to putting before ending off for the day.

Wednesday, the Pro-Am day, would be a light, unserious tuneup for Thursdays' opening round. During the tournament itself warmup and practice sessions were geared to shorter concentrated efforts with the emphasis on staying sharp and up for the day's round of golf and the rounds to follow during the tourney. Specific exercises for the back with emphasis on stretching were to be done two to three times a day. This was the routine that he consistently followed for success.

Each player may have a different routine or plan that he follows. That's fine; it should however be tailored individually. The vital thing is to adopt a plan of action based on what's the most workable routine that gets results and stick with it.

If your assessment reveals you're having trouble with your swing and its mechanics, then you should seek out or get with a good instructor to help you on this area or areas of technique and correct them.

Chapter VIII

Mental Toughness:
The Will to Succeed in Golf

Besides thinking big, and having worthwhile goals to shoot for, the successful golfer has learned to create a discipline that can effectively deal with the pressure of competition when it arises; this is a form of mental toughness that's vitally important. This quality is necessary if you're going to be the best player that you can be.

People in general react to situations in a number of ways. Some fearfully avoid or ignore conflict, others succumb to it, while others will elect to confront or attack the provocation. Golfers are no different.

It's my observation that in golf, the player who can turn a potential threatening crisis into an opportunity to score, is the one who confronts the situation and responds to the urgency of the scene and what's required to fix it, as if inviting a series of challenges to get him up to it, making it okay for such to happen.

It seems that for the pro, the occasioned bad shot chastises him to come back with even more determination on the next several shots. There's something to this in handling the current conditions, quickly reviewing the fundamentals and turning a potential negative situation into a positive one, instead of coming all apart and reeling off a series of mis-hit shots that cost him a good score. Challenges are the lifeblood that provide intensity and motivates the good player.

There's a lot to learn about the mental game, how the mind works, and how to be in control of it. This section of the book is intended to highlight the basic discoveries and laws concerning it. You need to become a better student of the mind game to play your best.

Where you're having trouble with concentration, feel burned out in your game, can't seem to manage yourself on the course and cause any real strategy, then you need help on the mental approach to the game and in regaining that mental toughness you once had as a player.

The Pre-Shot Mental Routine

There's an important law in golf that all players need to know about in order to have an effective mental approach and which has to do with the Pre-Shot Mental Routine every time you make a golf shot to the target.

There are a variety of reasons that result in a poorly played, mis-hit shot. I could roll out a long list of things that went wrong in some aspect of the physical swing and the mental thought process, yet these explanations merely state the effect of would-be indecision when shooting to the target.

This had been an intrigue to me as a player over the years in my own game and in observing that of others. I compared what a good player put his attention on in his game versus what a less competent player does.

The less experienced player has his attention more or less fixed on how to make the swing whereas the good player has his attention on the out-come and has the intention to make the shot happen. Having mastered the necessary skills, the professional or better player creates an atmosphere of confidence for himself to trust his skills and ability to produce the intended results; in other words he knows or expects it to happen, and it does rather routinely.

The better player has knowledge based on experience and familiarity with what causes a good shot, whereas the less able player to a greater or lesser degree doesn't know what caused good or bad shots, and is adversely affected by this lack of knowledge. He is likely to assign the wrong reason to his errant shot and will rather anxiously "buy" this and that, to quickly remedy the scene that is starting to unravel with all kinds of "band aid" solutions that he has heard of or adopted himself—which in most cases makes things even worse. Especially if he's out in the throes and thrashings of a round of golf.

The biggest difficulty and the deadliest of all sins that the golfer commits in his game is being *indecisive*.

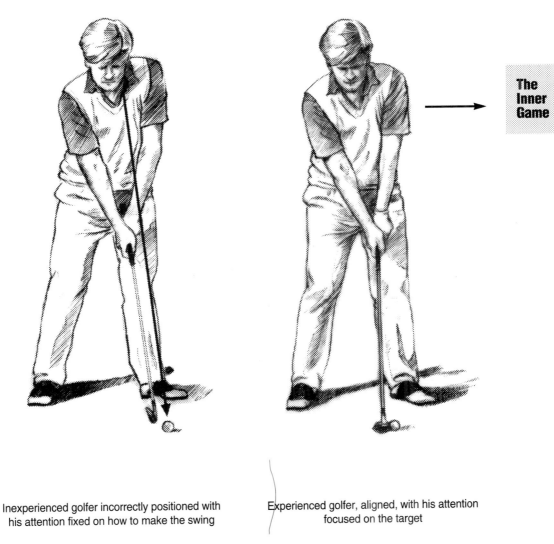

Inexperienced golfer incorrectly positioned with
his attention fixed on how to make the swing

Experienced golfer, aligned, with his attention
focused on the target

Indecisiveness shows itself in a number of way—in improper club selection, poor course management and strategy, lapses in concentration and mis-hitting the shot—accounting for more errant shots than any other factor in hitting a golf ball.

So we have a natural law about this:

> **ALL WELL EXECUTED GOLF SHOTS ARE THE RESULT OF BEING DECISIVE AND SURE AT THE MOMENT OF HITTING THE GOLF BALL**

And it's corollary:

> **ALL POORLY PLAYED GOLF SHOTS ARE THE RESULT OF BEING INDECISIVE AT THE MOMENT OF HITTING THE GOLF BALL**

All bad shots and their miscues reduce down to this law. Golf tournaments are won and lost due to this sole factor, indecision.

Indecision is the primary reason for mis-hits

The Masters and US Open Tournaments of the last several years are a good examples of this, over the last nine holes of play in the scores of those who are in contention for victory at the closing set of holes. This is where the tournament is won or lost coming down the final stretch.

The actual percentage of times a player is indecisive in a round of golf is rather interesting study that would most likely reveal some surprising insight into what goes through a player's mind as he encounters a variety of situations he must face.

Making a quick study of this, I would venture to say that a golfer, with all the variables and factors at hand, encounters approximately 1500 mental calculations alone having to do with hitting a golf shot in a span of four to five hours over eighteen holes. No wonder a golfer usually starts to tire on the back nine—not so much due to physical tiredness but more so to do with mental fatigue setting in.

If you find that you're being hesitant, doubtful and can't make up your mind on what shots to hit or find that your attention is too much on how you're going to hit the shot—then these add up to more or less confusions, which result in an indecisive effort and less effective shots to the target.

You'll have better scores if you play each shot being more decisive in what you're going to do and in doing it then and there, eliminating all the other clutter and less important aspects of shot-making. You have to adopt a central idea that results in a motion directed towards an intended target or objective. This can be whatever you make it to be, swing key[47] or any particular thought that is communicated personally in such a way that's simple to do and is proven to work for your game.

Some keys have been to: "take it back low and slow," "extend it back," "hook up the swing," "sweep it back," "keep your eye on the ball," "stay down and through," "listen for the sound of the ball coming off the club-head or putter," "be decisive," "make the shot," "trust your swing," "let it fly"... and others, etc..

These are all effective because they get the golfer to carry out his thought into a motion (shot). These keys will reduce the confusion and will produce a higher percentage of decisive shot-making and will boost one's confidence overall.

47. swing key: predominant thought or idea to make the swing

Golfer going over his notes of swing keys

One should be well above 50% of his shots in decisiveness; 90% approximates the ideal, in order to effectively score at the game of golf. Below this figure the golfer is guessing and figuring out way too much what to do, instead of having a plan to just execute the shot. In other words, instead of just hitting the ball with some authority the golfer becomes bound up thinking too much (over the ball) about the mechanics of the shot.

The good player in contrast has learned that the key to a good shot has to do with being sure and creating a sense of concentration. He also has learned to trust his instincts and play the shot in front of him with a sense of a "controlled abandon," and isn't afraid to just go with the shot; this is aggressiveness in a causative[48] sense that you hear a lot about.

This is why the golf game that you encounter on the course is such a challenge and is so different from hitting balls to a target at the range. The

48. causative: effective

150

course presents eighteen holes of varying degrees of difficulty of actual changing shots and challenges that the golfer must confront and deal with. This happens on a continuous basis: having to consider a number of factors that must be figured out and decided on a given shot, being subject to mental errors in attitude and to lapses in concentration, miscalculations in yardage, temperature, wind velocity, altitude, etc..

Here's a scale that gives you an approximation of the relationship between Decisiveness/Indecisiveness and the potential strokes gained and/or lost from such an important mental factor that this plays in your game.

As you can see from this scale, being decisive in your game will produce better scores, and where you find yourself being indecisive more times than not, your game will suffer and you'll reach less potential in your golf.

DECISIVENESS/INDECISIVENESS SCALE PERCENTAGE

Gain/Lost	to Score	Rating
80% – 100%	10 to 15	Excellent
60% – 80%	8 to 12	Good
40% – 60%	4 to 7	Fair
20% – 40%	1 to -5	Poor

Chapter IX

Golf is a Thinking Man's Game

The decisiveness scale is an important index in that it shows the role of intention and the degree to which the golfer uses a sound, effective mental approach. This index is tied directly to the golfer's ability to use such mental resources such as visualization, imagination, sound judgment and experience. The golfer who thinks the smartest and plays decisively is high on this scale and plays very close to his potential.

Where the golfer finds himself lower on this scale will most likely coincide with the areas of difficulty where he has stuck attention and finds it difficult to be decisive. If you take a moment to look specially at where you're having trouble in your shot-making, you are going to find areas where you lack confidence and the above respective percentages really comes into play.

Confidence, knowing that you can create an intended result, and decisiveness,[49] carrying through one's intention in a totally positive way, carrying through that intention in a determined way, operate together in a close relationship and are necessary teammates to one another in golf's mental approach. They are important components in producing results in mastering the mental game.

Every golfer comes to realize the importance of this with the inner game approach. He is looking for a better way to improve on it, yet he has usually looked in the wrong places for the answers.

What works with the successful player is to redirect his attention more onto the feel of the swing in a mental way. I get him to focus on getting

49. decisiveness: the act or condition of being decisive; sure

ready, set, and commencing firing the shot to its respective target; in other words, I get him to make a decisive motion in executing the shot.

This is the frame of mind that each shot requires and it has its own precise series of steps which define a mental routine setting the swing in motion from its decision point and carrying it through to its execution in a controlled, consistent effort.

The Role of Attention and Intention

There are two chief mental components that the good player intuitively uses that add up to proven success in their shot making. These are Attention and Intention.

Intention is a very important mental component in the hitting of the golf shot to a given target. Every endeavor that you take on involves intention. It's the basic, common denominator to golf or any activity where a mental approach is required as an action. Without it nothing is accomplished.

In sports such as golf that involve a high degree of mental calculations and decisions, the athlete is constantly confronted with barriers and obstacles in making the correct choices in the estimation of effort required to get the job done. The quarterback in football has to think smart and overcome the obstacles presented by the opponent, stick to a proven strategy or change to a more decisive one right at the line of scrimmage. Race car drivers likewise are confronted with a vast panorama of changing barriers and obstacles demanding split-second decision making or face impending death.

The golfer is making many decisions about which shot-making skill and strategy he will have to use. He has to be working constantly in the direction of seeing it happen and want to bring about the given result; this is intention. It's the carrier wave that produces the intended result.

There is a natural law that has to do with this:

> INTENTION IS ALWAYS SENIOR[50] TO MECHANICS.
> THE QUALITY OF THE GOLF SHOT DEPENDS ON THE AMOUNT OF
> DECISIVENESS PRESENT AND IS THE DIRECT RESULT OF
> THE GOLFER'S DEGREE OF INTENTION

50. senior: higher in importance

Attention is the mental component of focusing on a particular object. In golf this boils down to basically locating the green or hole to hit to, with the intention to produce the result over there at the target.

This is a rather basic fundamental that is often overlooked by even the advanced player—many times his focus on the target has shifted too much to the ball. The primary focal point has become the ball, instead of the target.

The primary focus must be directed towards the hole or target on the course; this is of utmost importance to the golfer as it keeps the intention going and needs to be part of his pre-shot routine to a given target (the pre-shot routine is discussed in more detail in the next chapter of this section).

The target is the primary focal point

In other sports, the athlete is able to focus directly at the target, whereas in golf the player approaches the target from a sideways position, not facing a target directly with his body.

The golfer has to place his attention on finding the proper alignment and address position instead of focusing on the target or hole in front of him. This is particularly a problem for the beginner and the average golfer as their sole attention becomes absorbed in getting aligned to the ball and on how they can make the swing itself.

On the other hand, the good player has more available attention focused on the target of what he is intending to reach, which is a shot close to the target or in the hole.

In observing the process with countless good players there was a common thread: the golfer's attention needed to be simultaneously on the primary focus, the target, and the ball, the secondary focus point. In other

Golfers attention focused on the the ball and the target.

words he has blended his focus as one with the ball and target.

Top players like Bobby Jones, Ben Hogan, Greg Norman, Raymond Floyd, Jack Nicklaus, and Tom Watson, to name a few that come to mind, shift their attention back and forth from the target to the ball, and exemplify this by starting the backswing immediately upon seeing the hole (again) in their primary focus to the target.

Any delay from this spontaneous process interrupts the feel of the shot and the concentration on the target and lessens their chances for a good shot. Bobby Jones commented in his book, *Golf Is My Game*, "It is far easier to maintain a complete relaxation (prior to swinging) if one keeps continually in motion... Whenever I hesitated or took a second waggle I could look for trouble".[51] This is vitally important to grasp in hitting well executed shots and establishing a sound workable pre-shot mental routine.

Therefore there is a law having to do with this in golf's mental approach:

THE TARGET IS THE GOLFER'S PRIMAY FOCAL POINT OF ATTENTION. THE BALL IS THE PRIMARY FOCUS OF MECHANICS. ATENTION IS THEN SELECTIVELY SHIFTED BACK AND FORTH FROM THE TARGET AS ITS PRIMARY FOCUS AND THE BALL AS ITS SECONDARY FOCAL POINT. BOTH BECOME ONE IN FOCUS IN THE EXECUTION OF HITTING THE BALL TO THE TARGET.

51. *Golf Is My Game,* by Bobby James

Chapter X

How You Play—It's the Thought That Counts!

Playing golf can be broken down into two major parts: mental thought and physical movement. How you play is determined by the interaction of the these factors: thought, and movement in your shot-making.

When you come to a shot during your game, you size it up from your experience of hitting such shots (movement that you've experienced), you formulate an idea (thought) on how to hit this shot this time (movement/thought) and you hit or execute the shot (movement again). Your thought or idea and your degree of confidence in how you execute the shot determines its outcome.

Obviously, if your estimation of effort is correct, that is, it matches the set of factors such as: how the club performs, your swing tempo and rhythm, the right shot to hit and how hard, wind velocity and direction if present and so on, you'll play extremely well.

If your idea doesn't fit one or more of these factors or is negative, then you'll most likely make mistakes, have problems with some aspect of your pre-shot mental routine or swing and find yourself confused or out of control in your game. This adds up to the inconsistencies in one's golf.

Not all of us can of course approximate the levels of competence displayed by the pros but we can surely learn the winning approach that they use. There is no actual attainable absolute in golf, yet each of us will play better by eliminating the confusion, the negative considerations that breakdown this coordination between thought and movement.

Here's a drill that will help when it comes to this.

Get the idea of making a pitch or chip shot to a target or hole. This is intention. Find a target that interests you and pitch the ball (motion) to the target or hole without getting into thinking too much; just pitch a number of shots this way getting into the motion of it and doing it. Continue doing this exercise to the point that you can do it without effort and are more in tune with the motion of the shot, instead of getting too mechanical about it.

Now take a longer shot say with a seven or eight iron and work up to hitting more shots in a comfortable way just flowing to the target as a motion instead of thinking while you swing; let go of all the thinkingness[52] and just go with a flowing motion and let the shot go to the target. Get the feeling of walking into the shot and letting it go to the target with ease and no built up tension.

Golf is two games in one: the mental process of turning thoughts (intention) into physical motions (action). The swing itself is the execution of the thought or idea into the playing field (the golf course) that you envision.

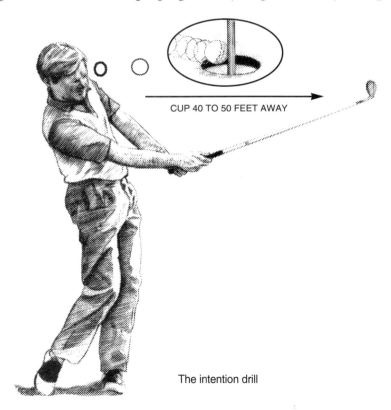

CUP 40 TO 50 FEET AWAY

The intention drill

52. thinkingness: thinking too much with the mechanics of the swing or shot

Each shot that you bring about is a conscious effort derived from your intention to make it happen. Every action that you make is actually decided in some form before its execution. Where that intention is clear-cut and decisive, then the outcome will most likely be a good shot.

There is really no such thing as hitting the shot on "automatic" without thinking about it. That's not true. The ease with which the professional hits his shots gives the apparency that this is the case. Each shot is hit with some degree of intention present although he may only have a small amount of attention on the process while he's doing it, due to his familiarity with the shot. This is similar to what you do in driving to work or the store every day—this is something that you just do without a lot of thinking involved.

The mental routine or key that I mentioned before is all-important. It incorporates each of the necessary components (attention, intention, focusing) and is the one thing that all good players of the game have in common, that they consistently use. You most likely have some sort of mental routine in your own game even though you may not be aware of it. The pros are best at doing this for success in golf.

Chapter XI

The Secret That The Pros Use

This pre-shot routine is vitally important in the execution of good golf shots because it is the key thing that the golfer does in setting up the *feel* of the shot before hitting to the target. This routine involves more than just getting aligned to the target, with the golfer's stance, which is a necessary factor of course, but is a focusing of mind and body to bring about the execution of the golf shot at its highest point of decisiveness and feel.

The good golfer relies on this sense of feel and uses it as a mental key to visualize a successful shot to the target ahead of time. The golf shot is thought of as a Cycle of Action[53] that flows from start to finish to the target and to the next shot.

Let's break down the components of this routine and examine each part. First there's the word routine. The American Heritage Dictionary defines the following: routine—noun: 1) a prescribed and detailed course of action to be followed regularly; a standard procedure. 2) a set of customary and often mechanically performed procedures or activities. Mental—adjective. 1) having to do with the mind, for the mind. Intellectual. Pre-shot—adjective. 1) before the execution of the shot.

When we combine all the meanings, we have a concept that is an unvaried action from shot to shot with a prescribed sequence of actions.

The Pre-shot Mental Routine

The Pre-shot Mental Routine prepares the golfer for the shot to come, gives the necessary sense of feel, and provides an image of the shot at hand

53. cycle of action: the sequence that an action goes through, wherein the action is started, continued, and then completed. [Taken from *The Problems of Work,* by L. Ron Hubbard]

that the player can visualize and then bring about the execution of the swing that's right for that situation.

This routine, to use a simple example, is very much like the shifting of the gears on your automobile. When you shift the gears correctly in the proper sequence, the car continues to move forward in a smooth transition from one gear to the next with the driver in full control of his automobile.

Assuming that the pre-shot mental routine has prepared the golfer with a well thought-out and rehearsed shot that he can perform with some ease,

The Pre-shot Mental Routine

the action phase of hitting the golf shot is readied for "launching." Without this smooth transition in the cycle of action in your game, you run the risk of trying to "drive the car" to its intended target without going through the necessary "pre-drive" procedures.

This major phase of the shot, the pre-shot routine, according to good players can amount to as much as 50–75% of the effort involved in hitting good golf shots. The majority of players feel that such a routine also brings about better concentration for them as it provides a pattern that they can use as a key in good shot-making.

The Pre-shot Routine: How It Can Work For You

The Pre-shot Routine used by the pros works like this.

Purpose: To teach the golfer the importance of a pre-shot mental routine, and to establish, maintain, and effectively use such in his game.

Step 1: SURVEY. The first step in good shot-making is surveying what's required of the shot at hand. This requires perceiving the actual conditions

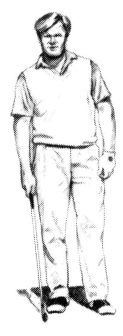

The Survey step of the Pre-shot Mental Routine

165

such as the lie of the ball, stance, target (pin position or placement for the next shot), and obstacles to the target (water, out of bounds, sand, rough, wind, altitude, condition of the landing area, grass etc.).

There is a mental checklist that programs all necessary data into the mind's computer (type of lie, distance, target dimensions, temperature, wind velocity, etc.) Drill this Survey part of the routine now, where you actually go through the steps of studying the target, gathering all the appropriate data so that you have the correct data to evaluate with and are ready to proceed to the next step of the routine. You should find yourself forming a conclusion in regard to that process. This leads us to the next phase, the decision-making process.

The Decide step of the Pre-shot Mental Routine

Step 2: DECIDE. Every golf shot that you hit is programmed to achieve a specific result based on the information you have given the mind—the quality of that decision is relative to the quality of the information given to it.

Having perceived the actual conditions you can now decide on the direction and shape of the shot and finally select the club. Once the decision has been made it should be reviewed against its potential for success—your degree of proficiency in making that kind of shot.

If you do not feel decisive or confident with the shot that you have selected, go back and redo Step #1, surveying for a new shot that you feel has a greater potential for success. You will arrive now at "your best shot."

This can also be drilled and should be, as the importance of the outcome of the golf shot hinges around this one factor—coming to a decision about the type of shot you are about to hit. This is a mental exercise that is a part of developing a good pre-shot routine in your game.

You can drill this part of the routine by gauging your response to the following question: Did you come to a decision point and act upon it?

The Rehearse step of the Pre-shot Mental Routine

Step 3: REHEARSE. The next phase is taking that decision to get the ball in or close to the hole or target, and rehearsing the shot mentally. This is where you visualize the intended result of the shot at hand, "see it happen-

167

ing in your mind," "feeling the shape of the swing" necessary with all the correct data needed.

The practice swing allows the golfer to make a swing impression based on the input from the survey step and creative imagination gathered on the correct shot to hit. The better player can work out and shape the shot he is about to hit and rehearses the shot beforehand.

The rehearsal step can be drilled in the following manner: make a practice swing towards your intended target with either a full swing effort or a half to three-quarters swing, keying on the feel of the swing you're about to make. If you're shaping the shot in a particular fashion (either right to left or left to right) then program the swing for such and try to sense the feel of the specific swing motion required. Some players such as Lanny Wadkins and Ian Woosnam, who are more spontaneous and ready to fire the ball to the target, like to just fire the shot to the target and use, if any, an abbreviated practice swing to the target.

This is the precise series of steps in the technique of good shot-making, that if followed will get the golfer to focus on and concentrate on "doing what he's doing while he's doing it." And doing so will eliminate the majority, if not all, of the distractions that can enter the scene in hitting the ball to the target. At this point the golfer is ready to combine both the mental and physical components and execute—launch the shot to the target.

Ben Hogan and Jack Nicklaus are the best examples of concentration in their pre-shot mental routines along with golfing greats, Bobby Jones and Walter Hagen, from golf's golden era.

Step 4: EXECUTE. This is the moment of truth where all components of the pre-shot mental routine must come together and be coordinated for firing. The mental key of being decisive and the correct choice of shot to hit, combined with the swing key that the golfer is using.

The golfer now walks into the shot, and gets comfortably aligned with the target. He now directs his focus on hitting the shot to the intended target. This all happens rather quickly at this point as the ball is now driven to the target with a smooth, rhythmic, decisive swing of the club, the player expecting nothing but positive results.

End Result: A golfer who has a pre-shot mental routine that works for him in his game.

The post-execution phase of the routine—where the ball went and how close to the target it arrived goes through a feedback process in monitoring

The Execute step of the Pre-shot Mental Routine

The Inner Game

the results of the shot. The key question is basically: Was it a good, fair or bad shot? This can be evaluated and noted for one's next series of shots, after which one can note the trend in shotmaking and how well the golfer is being decisive with his golf shots for that day.

Changes can be entered in strategy based on this information. It's important for the golfer to be nothing more than analytical about evaluating his shotmaking, and I recommend using "The Wave Principle Triangle," (Balance, Rhythm, Tempo = Timing from Chapter VII of Section I) to use an effective system to note what was good or bad with the shot as you go on playing the course.

The final phase of the pre-shot mental routine, the execution phase, can be drilled in the following manner: Focus on carrying through, moving from "the thinking mode" of thought to "the hitting mode" of action—aligning all three Outer, Inner, and Strategy Game "keys" to one all encompassing one—

which is being Decisive and hitting the golf shot to the target in a well-timed swing motion. Learn to bring your focus, your state of mind to a peak of intensity and "pull the trigger".

Once you have learned each step of the routine and can now use it in your game, there's an additional drill that you can do to master it. Get an idea on how long it takes you to sequence through each step in hitting the ball without being rushed or in taking too much time. Hit several shots to the target. Have your instructor, a golfing friend, or even yourself using a stop-watch time how long it takes you to complete the pre-shot routine, from start to finish.

You will find that there is an average time that it takes you on each shot. This time is the optimum amount of time for you to take and when you deviate from it, taking less time or longer, you will not have as good, decisive shot-making in golf. Drill this routine hitting a series of shots to a given target with different clubs working on staying within this time element by several seconds either way. When your game is off you will find that your routine has been altered. This drill also works quite well in your practice putting.

The key point to remember here is to keep in a sense of motion and feel of the given shot. Move from one part of the sequence to the next with a good sense of rhythm and timing and you've got it! This will vary from person to person in the amount of time required, but shouldn't take more than a minute or so. If you take a longer amount of time then it's a good idea to walk faster between shots in an effort to allow you the extra time to complete this routine.

This precise Pre-shot Mental Routine allows the golfer to do his thinking in the correct phase and coordinate the action phase in the proper sequences in a more efficient manner.

You can learn and improve this routine for your own game. It's the one key thing that the pros do for success in their game. If you keep that specially in mind, you can learn the technique that will peak your ability to concentrate as much as 75% or better, that all good players have come to develop for success and that you too can have in your game!

Chapter XII

Concentration—
A State of Mind

Golfers describe concentration in many ways. Some define it while play-ing their best as "being totally focused," "in the zone," "totally there," "in the groove," "in the driver's seat," "in the flow"...etc.. Concentration is defined as a noun: close attention. Concentrate as a verb: to direct one's thoughts or attention; focus. [AMERICAN HERITAGE DICTIONARY].

All three of Golf's Outer, Inner, and Scoring Games depend on one key ingredient for success: Concentration. Without it the golfer will never reach the potential that he is capable of in playing in golf.

In studying the performances of good amateur and pro golfers, I found that besides being able to control the motion of the golf swing better, the good player is able to focus on his scoring game due to better concentration and target focus.

This heightened focus carries over to not only particular shot-making skills, but thinking with and working out strategies over several holes at a time; in other words their thought and actions were tied to both the present action of playing that particular shot and hole, and with that of future holes to be played. The good player just does it, without any hitches or complications.

The good player becomes aware of what works, and heightens that awareness in a state of mind that is more decisive and is thus freed up to put more attention on the target as he executes the golf shot to each intended target. Thus he is able to control the motion with certainty. This breeds con-fidence because the good player can do the necessary actions that produce good shots—this creates prediction which is the certainty of good shot-making, and allows the golfer to stay in the present and "create the moment" of the given shot.

Legendary golfer Bobby Jones, in his book, *Golf is My Game,* described the perception in his own words as follows, "To preclude any concern with the manner of swinging.... I liked to think of erecting a wall containing the ball and my left eye, and then focus my entire concentration upon producing the desired result on the other side of the wall. I wanted to leave my swing to take care of itself. Whenever I could achieve this detachment, my swing would slow down to its proper rhythm."

Although each of the better players who I coached had better and more efficient swings than their counterparts, the swing was ruled out as the sole source of failure and was found not to be the primary reason for lack of success in playing one's best. It actually proved out to be that the better the player, the more he was in control of that focus mentally and able to direct his attention, and focus on the execution of the swing and target at the same time. This focus specifically brings about a higher mental state needed to play effective golf.

In contrast, the average golfer has his attention mainly fixed more on how to hit the shot, and can't integrate all three parts of the game that are required in one's concentration. Less competent golfers simply have more failures at not being able to effectively sustain their concentration beyond the swing, and find that their focus breaks down more often than not in their mental approach in playing golf shots during an eighteen hole round. There's such a thing as concentrating too much on the swing and getting everything to work right.

Concentration is the all-important mental component to the game of golf and with other sports, yet it seems more crucial in its demands in golf because the player seemingly has to bring his mind to a heightened state of focus each time a golf shot is hit. Concentration stems from the intention to produce a given result.

In other sports, such as tennis and baseball, the opponent provides the stimulus for the player to respond to (the hitting of the ball), thus creating the action and motion of the shot, whereas in golf this is not the case—the golfer has to cause or initiate this interaction individually. The golf course itself "dictates" the action in a sense, but the golfer has to rely on and use a mental approach to not only make the correct choice of shots, but bring about each shot—this is where a prepared, pre-shot routine assists the player to "get up" for the given shot.

The golfer is on his own in this respect. It is in this mental approach to the game that there exists a difference in ability of players to tap the powers of the mind and concentration that are needed to play one's best. This division exists even at the top, amongst touring players, and is evidenced by those who finish consistently in the top twenty on the Tour each year.

Ben Hogan, Jack Nicklaus, Tom Watson, Gary Player, Steve Ballesteros, and Raymond Floyd are good examples of the intense concentration and state of mind needed to play the game to win.

Leading amateurs and pros describe concentration as a state of mind in which their attention becomes totally absorbed or focused on the task at hand, in which they are free from distraction, and are tuned into a heightened focus and intensity, to hit the ball to the intended target.

Jack Nicklaus exemplifies the ideal in golf's mental game, possessing a tremendous ability to concentrate and focus at a high level and state of mind. He seemingly has the ability to direct his attention at will onto the golf shot he is about to hit, and brings his intention to the highest degree of intensity, possibly more than any other player, except perhaps Hogan, in modern day golf, and Bobby Jones, in golf's golden era.

Good players have learned that the best way to develop, improve, and heighten concentration is through the use of a pre-shot mental routine. When used properly, it directs the golfer's attention from the conceptualization (intention) of the golf shot, to its execution (motion) to the target.

Golfers will find that their concentration breaks down in a particular phase of the pre-shot mental routine, and it's in this area that player will find that there is some indecision occurring that prevents a well executed golf shot to the target. For example, the golfer's focus is fixed on something having to do with the swing itself, its mechanics, or something to do with alignment, or the correct shot to hit due to changing wind conditions; it can be a combination of these things that essentially disperses the golfer's attention—these things cut short that focus onto just making the shot in an indecisive way.

Instead of moving from one step to the next in a movement of flow, the golfer neglects, or "short circuits," some part of the prior step that's now incomplete in the routine, and "hurries" into the next phase and hitches there, with the result of a poorly hit shot to the target.

173

Those players at the pro level are able to "find the zone" as they align each aspect of the game to a series of "keys" that package up the thought and movement into a routine. This allows them to have more focus on the target as their primary point of interest.

Concentration has to do with doing what you are doing while you are doing it, and not allowing outside or internal distractions cut or get in the way of the task at hand.

Percy Boomer in his book, *On Learning Golf*, perceived it in an interesting way, "Good golf, consistent golf, depends upon being able to shut out our mental machinery (with its knowledge of the difficulties of the shot, the state of the game, etc.) from those parts of us which play golf shots."[54]

This requires a discipline that the good golfer learns. You will find that there are certain things that distract you more than others. If you can eliminate these, you will make improvement in your shot-making and overall score. This can be worked on and drilled in practice sessions and then worked into your game.

Tension is the biggest threat to the golfer's concentration level, causing the golfer's attention to dissipate, and affects the data gathering and decision making process in shot-making and strategy choices. The golfer has to have a relaxed state of mind to direct his focus freely and tension can ruin that process of relaxation, which is necessary to perform one's best at golf.

The following is a concentration drill that I have devised for the players that I work with that will help in your golf game.

CONCENTRATION DRILL

Purpose: To improve the golfer's concentration in hitting the golf shot.

Emphasis: In this drill, the player fixes his attention onto some aspect of his golf swing, alignment, or pre-shot routine. He'll notice that when he does this, his attention goes to one or more of the above areas. This may be the clubhead, his takeaway position waist-high, or at the top of the swing.

He now directs his focus onto something more specific that he can find some interest in—the sweet spot of his driver, the left foot turned slightly outward towards the target, the belt position at waist-high position, etc..

He then shifts his attention onto some other part of his swing, alignment, or routine. This may be something like noticing the grip and how the

54. *On Learning Golf:* by Percy Boomer

hands feel working together as a unit, his set-up position, moving from his center back and through in a balanced swing, getting decisive about the swing and the shot to the target, etc..

Effective practice becomes an exercise in understanding the cause-effect relationship of what the club and body are doing, how the swing feels, how they blend together harmoniously in the golf swing, and the level of focus the golfer can direct to the shot at hand.

If your attention is too fixed on a particular aspect in doing this exercise then this is a point in your concentration that breaks down and will invite error in the execution of the swing to the target. If that is the case, then pinpoint what exactly is causing the hangup or get your instructor to help ascertain the difficulty. Look for tension, something that is misunderstood, or a fixed, false idea of swing technique that is being misapplied.

Part II: There is a second part of this drill that is geared towards practicing concentration in your shot-making either on the course or at the range.

Emphasis: In this part of the drill the golfer is to work up a series of shots to a given target. If you're at the range doing this drill then you will simulate playing several golf holes and shots to various targets as if it were an actual par four hole, par three, or par five hole, going through a variety of shots.

Start with hitting your tee shot to a target, then hit your second shot to the "green," and so on, paying particular attention on focusing on the target and using the pre-shot mental routine, directing your attention selectively back and forth from the ball to the target and hitting the ball to the target, moving from each part of the sequence to the next, in a smooth focused manner.

Work on perfecting a better tempo and routine and stay in a flow with this and you will find that your concentration will heighten and achieve more of a focus with the target.

End Result: A golfer who has an improved ability to concentrate and can direct that focus in hitting shots to the target.

I recall an article some years ago in one of the golf magazines, in which junior golfers in Japan were drilled on concentrating better. What their instructors did were to use loud sounding noises, hitting cans together with sticks, and talking in an effort to interfere and break the level of concentration of their students so that they would become accustomed to distractions and be able to handle such without these affecting their concentration. This drill improved their mental focus and ability to deal with distractions on the course.

This is something that you can also do with a golfing friend or your instructor and have him coach you on some of the areas that you're affected by, when it comes to your concentration. There are some golfers who have gotten so bad at this, they can't concentrate at all without scolding the entire foursome for practically breathing. They need to do an exercise like this to make it more enjoyable for themselves and the others around them in golf. Concentration gets a bad name when it is directly tied to getting too serious and fixed over the outcome of the shot.

A vital key to golf's mental approach centers around the ability to concentrate.

Chapter XIII

Mental Approach in Golf Drills—Section II

I've included here a series of drills that have been useful to golfers in improving their mental performance and ability to score better in golf. They are laid out on a gradient[55] that builds upon each other, yet can be done as a remedy by itself.

GETTING INTO ACTION/DECISIVENESS DRILL.

Purpose: The aim of this drill is to teach the golfer to look at the shot at hand and come to a quick decision about what to do and do it without deliberating too long over the ball; but to be decisive and get into action in hitting the shot to the target.

Emphasis: The training stress in this drill is on creating a golf motion from one's thought or intention and getting decisive in hitting the shot. The drill can be done at the driving range or out on the course in the following manner: the golfer approaches the shot in front of him and looks at the lie of the shot, decides on the shot at hand and either makes a free or actual swing to the target with or without the club based on that information. Stress is placed on having the golfer make a decision and to carry out that intention in the shot.

The golfer will find that when he comes to a self determined decision he will hit better, more confident shots to the target and he also will observe that where he is indecisive in his choices he will have more difficulty and lack of confidence, which results in poorer played golf shots.

The player, on each shot, must make this decision, come to his own con-

---

55. gradient: a gradual approach to something taken step by step

clusions, and make the shot at hand. Where he fails to do so, he will feel less in control and more the effect of his own indecision.

The golfer should make note of these indecisive areas and work on them to discover what part of his mental approach to the game is out and practice these areas newly, incorporating them into his pre-shot mental routine.

End Result: A golfer who can carry out an intention, be decisive and get into action of hitting golf shots with confidence .

SEEING THE SHOT GO TO THE TARGET/HOLE DRILL.

This drill teaches the golfer to visualize making the shot—the golfer perceives or gets the idea of the feel and sense of movement that is needed with the club and body through space on a given shot in making a swing to the target. This is the perception of kinesthesia.[56]

It's interesting to note that this perception differs amongst golfers; some have a relatively high degree of ability—you've heard the statement "he's got natural ability" all too often that refers to this—whereas in golfers that I have observed and worked with, at least fifty to sixty-five percent had difficulty in being able to visualize the golf shot in their mind to the target or hole. Some golfers operate more effectively on other perceptions, such as sound as a key.

Emphasis: In this drill the training stress is on the golfer learning to develop what I'll call here a "visual field of impressions" based on a sense of movement and feel. Based on the information given to it, the mind offers a solution of the correct estimation of the effort necessary to accomplish the plan, gets the body to execute the intention to perform the task of hitting the ball to the target with a physical movement, the swing.

This is where creative thought, imagination, and experience merge to produce a golf shot that is envisioned by the golfer, a shot close to the target. The golfer's experience comes heavily into play here in his shot-making skill and he'll find that he's more able to pull up and visualize shots where he has had successes than the times where he has had losses, difficulty, and confidence-eroding experiences.

The golfer hits his best shots when there's a spontaneous interaction of the mind and body; this is best accomplished by a sense of rhythm in

56. kinesthesia: the sensation of bodily position, presence or movement through spatial dimensions

movement that is instinctive. The movement requires more effort and become less productive when the swing is allowed to become too rigid, and mechanical; thus creating a robotic swing motion of the body.

The golfer is not a machine; he (through his mind) operates the body, and follows the laws of biomechanics of motion. The body mirrors the response of the mind's creation and carries out that swing motion in the physical universe.

The golfer will find that a musical rhythm closely approximating that of the tempo of the swing will be of great benefit to the golfer's sense of timing in keeping a consistent routine going in playing golf. Many key players of the game at the amateur and professional level use music not only to inspire themselves but also to keep the rhythm and timing going at a higher point of application (aesthetics).

This tune can be whatever you make it to be; when I was standout junior golfer coming up the ranks I matched up the beat of "Old Man River" with that of the image of Julius Boros's fluid swing motion. This was an insightful tip that I received from my dad, who was a champion golfer, that worked for me. This "music to one's swing" can vary as the emotional state of mind of the golfer is subject to change. Humming the tune works especially well in keeping a rhythm going as you're walking between shots and approaching the ball in the fairway.

One can also use action-sounding phrases that get the golfer into motion with the swing. Some examples of this are: "back and through," "low and slow," "one and two," "sweep it back and through," etc..

The golfer also will find that his swing has a certain beat to it that can be worked out into a pattern such as: one and two (hit), one, two, and three (hit). This is a good sensory key that can be used to maintain your proper pace especially when playing under the stress of competition.

End Result: A golfer who can create the idea of the shot in his mind and communicate that idea of the swing to the body with the right amount of effort and feel required to hit the golf shot.

"WALK INTO THE SHOT"/THE PRE-SHOT
MENTAL ROUTINE DRILL

Purpose: The aim in this drill is to train the golfer to recognize, know, and be in control of the cycle of action in hitting the golf shot. There is a precise sequence of actions that the golfer routinely follows in executing the golf shot.

It was found that one of the chief differences observed between the good player, pro, and the not-so-good average golfer is that the good player knows the importance of having a routine that he follows and doesn't deviate from because he knows that it is what works in producing a good shot. He knows that the routine is successful in that it acts as the packaging of all the keys both physical and mental into their proper sequential order, readied for launch to the target.

The pre-shot routine that is covered in full detail earlier in this section is an all-encompassing drill that incorporates all the swing keys of The Outer Game approach, especially those of alignment, getting comfortably set to the target, the Mental keys of The Inner Game/Mental Approach, the "Getting into Action/Being Decisive Drill" along with the "Seeing the Shot Going to the Target" (visualization), and lastly the Strategy keys (not yet covered) of executing the golf shot itself to the target from the last section of *The Ultimate Game of Golf* book. All these drills unite and come together in this all important routine in hitting the shot to the target.

Emphasis: In this drill the golfer pays particular attention to creating each part of the actual sequence of the routine: 1) surveying the shot; 2) coming to a decision on how to make it; 3) rehearsing the shot in one's mind (making a picture of the swing), and making a practice swing to the target, and 4) letting it go (execution) to the target.

These are the basic steps that you need to drill over and over to the point that you can do the routine without having to think about it. You'll also find that when you have the routine down and it's working for you in your game that there is a smooth transition from each phase to the next with a sense of motion.

You'll get more out of your practice sessions if you work on this, as it is this routine that goes astray out on the course during play where you control the shot-making process. Each player will find that his routine becomes his own with particular attention on one or more of its parts.

The golfer can compare scores with and without the pre-shot routine. Each golfer should review his pre-shot routine on a periodic basis and work this into his golfing fundamentals. Jack Nicklaus, Curtis Strange, Greg Norman, and Nick Faldo are excellent examples of the pre-shot mental routine in action—bringing their powers of concentration to the highest point of execution. If you're not sure about your own routine then get the watchful eye of your golf instructor to help you groove-in yours.

End Result: A golfer who has established a pre-shot mental routine that works for him resulting in improved mental performance.

DIRECTING YOUR ATTENTION DRILL

Purpose: The whole idea in this drill is to learn to direct your focus on each step of the pre-shot routine of the shot to be played, and bring that intention to its highest point in hitting shots to the target.

Emphasis: In this exercise the stress is in learning to go through the pre-shot mental routine and bringing your intention in hitting the golf shot to its highest state of concentration without being distracted. This is accomplished by having a clear picture of the shot that needs to be played, and in coming to a decision point (Step 2: Decide) of the Pre-Shot Mental Routine, which creates the motion and called-for action in the execution (Step IV: Execution) of the swing to the target.

The player will find that when the sequence is done correctly, that he's moving through each part of the routine in a concentrated state of mind, is focused on the shot to hit, and hits the shot in a spontaneity of motion and action.

Directing one's attention and getting decisive about the shot to be played is an essential part of the pre-shot mental routine. The golfer will find that his shots come off best when he's focused and can readily direct his attention through each phase of the routine.

End Result: Being able to bring your focus to its highest point of concentration and being decisive in hitting a golf shot to its target.

THE WHAT TO DO WHEN DISTRACTED/RELOADING DRILL

Purpose: To teach the player what he can do when distracted in hitting the ball, and how he can remedy this.

During the course of a round there will be distractions, lapses in concentration and basically moments when you are not ready to make the shot to the target. This will vary in each round of golf that you play, due to a number of factors such as your mental state that day, being in the present, how much attention you have on your game, etc..

Being in present time[57] is all important. Being in the now, allows the player to concentrate fully on the shot at hand. He has more attention "units" to use. He's in a higher state of mind, as he can direct his attention on what he's doing while he's doing it, and get more actions done more easily.

It's quite difficult to play up to your full potential if your mind is fixed on upsets or disturbing news, a lingering doubt about that three-putter you jabbed on the fourth hole, or an upset with your wife or business associate just before you have to tee up in a tournament. Anyway, it always seems that there is something that interferes with your golf as a distraction; especially so when you're not playing well. That's why you hear so much about concentration being a problem for golfers in their game; it becomes dispersed. Players can't direct their attention readily and stay focused.

These situations can be numerous where the golfer is being indecisive and can't pull the trigger or pulls the trigger impulsively without thinking it through and getting into action via a routine—the golfer needs to recognize this when it is happening and know what to do.

Emphasis: Here's what works best. The golfer needs to back off the shot and realize that regardless of what's the source of the distraction, he merely has had a break in his level of concentration; in other words it's been interfered with and the best solution to this is to simply regroup and "reload" the golf shot, not to worry about the source of the distraction. This can appear to be harder than it is as many golfers find themselves compelled to go ahead and hit the shot anyway.

There will be times where you can get away with this, but I don't advise it, because on the whole, you'll pay the price of an errant golf shot—it gets you in more trouble than if you were to start the process again with your

57. present time: the time which is now

182

pre-shot routine. Cycle through it again as if you were looking at this shot for the first time. You can shorten the routine to some degree because you are familiar with the shot at hand, but you must be careful with this in that you can get a little too careless with the shot.

You don't want to just mechanically go through the motions—you want to create the shot again in your mind's eye, get the idea of the shot going to the target effortlessly and bring your level of concentration to its highest for each shot. This requires discipline and learning to program the proper motor skill and response to the situation; the pros are by far the best at this and have learned to do so through hard-won experience.

Particular attention should be on developing a routine in which the golfer can experience being distracted and when so, use the above as a remedy to make the shot after all. This can be done as a drill where the golfer notices that his attention has been interrupted and quickly moves into the necessary remedy to handle it effortlessly and with confidence.

This works better in a practice session out on the course. It's not uncommon for the pros during a round to "reload the shot" several times. I've seen players back off the shot as many as eight to twelve times during a given round.

End Result: A golfer who has learned that when distracted, how he can remedy this, regroup, and replay an effective shot to the target.

WHEN IT'S ALL GOING WRONG/REGROUP DRILL

Now there is another non-optimum situation: when it's all coming apart and nothing will work in your game to remedy the crisis. This can go on for an indefinite period of time with the golfer at wit's end, uptight, and utterly frustrated about his game.

Obviously the golfer's game has hit the skids, "the wheels have come off" and his game is in for a big slump, leaving the golfer feeling helpless in his futile attempt to correct what's wrong. Each of us has been in this predicament most likely a number of times throughout the golf season and in our involvement with the game.

When being uptight in a difficult circumstance and when experiencing negativity, feeling stressed-out, and indecisive in their game, what I found that works with my players is this: the golfer should back off from hitting the ball and regroup his efforts newly, going through the entire pre-shot routine again as the focal point and remedy. It is okay to back off the shot, get refocused and begin again when you find yourself not ready to make a decisive swing. Forget what you think others are thinking about on this.

Here is some theory on this. It will be found that the golfer has had his attention fixed too heavily on something else besides the primary objective—the target itself. Reactive, negative input gains "air time" and control of the golfer's decision-making process, demanding inappropriate solutions that are not analytical.

Reactive solutions are not based on analytical data. Here's an example from one player's game, who was just three strokes off the lead in a tournament, when he played the thirteen hole. "I had just hit my tee shot out of bounds, and at this point found myself in a sudden rage.... I felt like a time bomb about to explode.... I didn't care where the next one (shot) was going to go.... I just felt compelled to hit it as hard as I could." It was the only "solution" that I could accept. It too went out of bounds, and there went the tournament for me."

Another player's solution to his dilemma happened in his club championship, which he was playing quite well in, and in contention, when on the par five seventh hole, an easy birdie hole, his third shot, a well hit wedge, hit below the hole, but failed to hold, and ended up about twelve feet above the pin. Being above the hole was not the place to be on this green. He knew that he needed to make this putt or face a longer putt on his next. He cringed as his putt slipped by the hole, and ended up some twenty feet below the hole, from where he felt a sick feeling well-up in his stomach. He promptly three-putted from there to his dismay.

It was ironic he said, as he recalled it, that as he approached the wedge shot, he started to feel nervous about the pin placement, and rightly so, as this is where he had four-putted the last time he'd played here in the tournament... He remembers feeling apprehensive, and thinking negative, and saying to himself, "Don't blow this Club Championship again, you dummy. Whatever you do, don't get above the pin here on this green 'cause you can easily four putt from there," which he did.

As you can see in these examples, each player had his attention stuck on a negative, reactive "solution" to his situation, and is compelled to act out or dramatize[58] the content of the bad experience.

58. dramatize: to repeat in action what has happened to one in experience. It's being replayed out if its time and period [From *Dianetics and Scientology Technical Dictionary*]

These "solutions" are charged with negative emotions and attitudes that "remind" the golfer of failure and loss. This can heavily affect the golfer's confidence level and flood emotions to the various systems of the body that come into play, resulting in a more restrictive golf swing.

The body mirrors the conflict of the mind. The body becomes tense. This is then manifested in a rigid swing or stroke. When one's confidence is undermined, there is always the tendency to rely on emotion as the solution and many golfers will look to mechanics as the physical way to fix the mental, which won't work. It will work with some players some of the time, but most often won't be the needed remedy.

This phenomena causes a breakdown in concentration as the golfer's attention disperses, and his state of mind is disturbed; he is upset with himself, his game, and the world around him! The longer he sits in the upset, the more he protests not wanting to play under such conditions. This will go on until he finds a way to accept what has happened (a bad shot or series of bad shots), or when the matter is rectified to his satisfaction with an acceptable shot.

Emphasis: The remedy and the way to handle this is to first of all be willing to accept a bad shot or series of bad shots. Too many golfers are resisting at all costs hitting a bad shot, and their attention is fixed on preventing a bad shot instead of producing a good one. So when you are playing don't be overly concerned with hitting bad shots, as you will hit a number of these each time you play. Bobby Jones knew the importance in this and knew each time he was to play a round of golf that he would realistically hit five bad shots or more a round.

Concentrate on the pre-shot routine and getting decisive about the shot to the target. Back off the shot when you aren't set due to whatever the reason, and direct your attention on being decisive with the shot and just do it.

There are many situations in shot-making that can be complex, and confusing, and throw you off, in indecision. The golfer will benefit from this drill and will have no concern on what acts as a distraction and will learn that he can deal with a variety of situations with a proven remedy that works for him in his game.

End Result: A golfer who is not the effect of distractions, lapses in concentration and can regroup his focus, resulting in a decisive shot to the target.

Chapter XIV

Golf's Inner Secret to the Scoring Game

No part of golf is as important as putting and its role in the mental game of golf. More leads are squandered away, charges made, leads changing hands than with any other club. More tourneys are won or lost with the putter than with any other club in the bag! Putting either creates a good score or denies one! Putting performance depends on your State of Mind!

A good putter cashes in on opportunities on the greens whereas the poor putter doesn't. A swing of four to ten strokes can potentially occur alone in the scoring strokes department! The Tour leaders in events won and money standings are all excellent, exceptional putters. Nicklaus, Watson, Player, Trevino and a host of other golfing greats were more than great ball strikers—they were great putters under pressure, averaging twenty-seven to twenty-eight putts per round.

PUTTING = SCORING!

A golfer may drive for show, but he putts for dough!

This brings to mind the story of one golfing great, Bobby Locke, who many consider one of the best putters of all times. Locke, back in the 1940's defeated Sam Snead eleven out of twelve times in a series of one-on-one exhibitions of brilliant putting performances in South Africa, and went on to devastate the American tour with his putter. He hit the ball right to left with a big sweeping hook, had a bad swing and grip, yet could putt like a magician on the greens.

187

Confidence and the ability to putt well under pressure is golf's most highly-prized jewel. Putting is that vital part of the game that accounts for almost fifty percent of your total scoring strokes and in which you can bring even the 300 yard drivers to their knees on the greens.

Chapter XV

The Mental Approach in Putting

Back in the days when I was a highly regarded junior player, my dad considered me the finest putter that he had ever seen. He had seen me hole a lot of putts then, long ones and shorts ones, from any angle and from all over the green. I was shooting in the seventies before I was eleven then, and was winning a lot at golf. I was confident that I could dispose of any worthy opponent on the green, which I did. He was right about my ability with the putter—no one ever got the title from me and I was the best then.

I recall one afternoon as I was practicing putting for a junior event one of the older players came over. He took a position about ten feet away, putter in hand, after observing me sink some "routine" eight to ten footers. He wanted to know what it was that I thought about in my putting and what was my "secret." He was hoping presumably for that special tip that would revitalize his slumping, rather beyond repair putting game.

Expecting some golden rule on the mechanics of putting, such as how to use the hands and wrists, keeping the head steady through the stroke, etc., to his dismay and chagrin, I proceeded to instruct him on the value of focusing his attention mentally on making the putt at present, getting the feel instead of all the negatives and considerations on not making the putt.

Asking Mr. Jensen to hole a five footer was like giving a death sentence to this man, as his body would tighten up on command. I told him this: "It appears to me that you have got the idea or a picture of some sort that makes you think negatively about your chances of making putts, and it continues to haunt you like a dark cloud every time you putt. You have gotten yourself convinced that you are a bad putter. You can't do that. You've got to trust your stroke and work on a simple one that allows you to feel where your hands need to go towards the hole."

Feel the Stroke

Feel the stroke and be confident in making it happen. I simply look at the hole and feel my way there and I get the idea of the ball going in the hole. I really don't think about it, I just see it in my "mind's eye." I'm totally positive about it going in, there isn't any thought to the contrary and it just does go in most of the time! Sometimes I'm distracted from someone else who is moving around or making noise on the green, but even with this I quickly return to focusing on the putt to hole. Putting to me is all feel and sensing the line to the hole.

Golfers who putt badly are in a mental slump of negative thinking, and definitely lack confidence. Their attention is stuck or too heavily absorbed by some aspect of the stroke itself and its mechanics. The golfer now introverts on his putting woes, and is thinking negative.

Stance and Alignment

The putting stroke should feel right. There are two sides to this: One is technique and the other is mental. The mechanics of the stroke need to be sound with a good set-up position in which the head and body remain fixed with little to no movement.

The eyes are over the ball and the body is aligned in a comfortable position looking in direct line to the hole. There is a little more weight on the left side to ensure a firm stroke is completed to the hole.

The Stroke

The hands and wrists work together in a back and through manner to the hole with a fluid, rhythmic motion, like a pendulum. The stroke is smooth and firm. The back of the left hand is firm at impact and doesn't break down. You want a repeating stroke, a motion back and through, that's consistent and on line to the hole. Let either your shoulders and arms or the hands control the stroke.

The majority of missed putts are due to the stroke breaking down at impact. This is where the right hand jerks or hits at the ball too forcibly and the left wrist fails to continue its motion to the hole. This breakdown is caused by two main faults: improper alignment to the hole, and mental pressure which forces the stroke to become too tense and rigid.

Putting is Chiefly Feel

Putting is chiefly feel, a solid foundation in alignment, and a firm back and through, fluid motion to the hole. The ball itself, when struck with a firm stroke will roll truer to the hole and will go in more often than a poorly hit putt. Mis-hit putts veer more off line and have less chance of going in especially in shorter putts. This is caused by twisting of the putterblade at impact which throws off the blade from being square to the line of the hole. The stroke in most cases has become too wristy when this happens. More and more Tour players are using a shoulder and arm stroke motion, which keeps the putterblade more on line throughout the stroke and is less tension producing.

When the stroke goes sour and becomes chronically bad, it's usually a combination of faulty mechanics and a mental lack of confidence in making the stroke.

Stress starts to build up in the golfer's mind. Analytically, the mind is looking for ways to handle "the problem of a faulty putting stroke that's gone bad." It scans for solutions from its various memory banks labeled Re: "Putting"—looking for the right data to correct the stroke." It gives the golfer bits and pieces of data from its files contained in the memory banks of "Putting Mechanics" and "Putting Experiences."

Along with this however, he gets files from the memory bank that contain negative experiences in picture form—upsetting memories, failures, and negative attitudes and emotions about the subject of putting. The player may or not be conscious of these painful pictures, as the reactive part of the person's mind operates below the person's awareness level.

These experiences are subjective, having to do with what has happened to the golfer as a putter, and his reactions to these experiences. They are tied to the reactive part of the mind (as earlier stated in Section II)—putting is now associated with something stressful. When it's time to putt or even as the golfer begins to approach the green he begins to tense up to the unpleasant fact that he's got to putt. He now has a queasy feeling about having to putt. He's more apprehensive. He's more concerned with the consequences of missing the putt and the next short one. He senses that he's going to make a "bad" stroke and proceeds to do so.

The more that he tenses up and resists making a bad stroke the worse the situation can become. The reactive input takes over, overrides the analytical part of the mind, and controls the scene forcing the player to make a less than ideal stroke.

Many golfers try to block out the negative stuff, instead of placing more attention on freeing up the stroke to the hole and getting the intention back into it. They end up instead resisting the thought of a bad putt and its consequences, which actually places more attention onto it (the negative)!

Along with this, the golfer's emotional response to putting and everything associated with it lowers from being interested in the putt as an opportunity to score well, to a mixed association of negative attitudes of antagonism, anger, hostility towards it, as well as the lower emotions of grief, despair, and apathy concerning it.

He now is focused more and more on it as a problem and has adopted any solution or "fix" to try to change this chronic or acute condition, losing more focus on the proper mental approach to putting which focuses more on the hole (target) using a stroke that is confident, trustworthy and built on a sense of touch and feel with the cup.

The Pre-putt Routine

Good putters have a routine that they employ to make all the right components in the stroke mesh and work together. This routine is very similar in approach to the pre-shot mental routine used in the rest of your game except on Step 1(Surveying the Shot)—you'll be gathering data of several key factors having to do with the putt itself: The direction of grain[59], the slope or angle of break, and the correct estimation of speed of putt.

These factors then dictate a decision to act on which is then rehearsed with a practice stroke along the intended line to the hole with emphasis placed on a smooth rhythmic stroke as a "key" for feel in the putting stroke.

Knowing what's now required and having worked out the exact stroke and line needed, the mental fundamentals quickly and spontaneously go to work with the stroke providing a heightened concentration on bringing off the intended result, the ball going into the hole!

1

2

3

4

The Sequence in the Pre-putt Routine

59. grain: the texture of the grass

Stroke the Putt with Your Mind's Eye.

There is a constant interaction occurring between the (mental) intention of the stroke and it's motion (physical) that is being fine-tuned and fed back to the mind, stroke and hands. Each works together as a unit.

Once the setup and alignment steps are done and the putt has been run through a practice run or two the mind takes over, visualizing the perfect speed and angle of the putt going in the hole. The mental key takes over and the stroke is decisively made to the hole with the idea of it going in.

The intention of the ball going into the hole is of primary importance and must be created and kept throughout the routine and the actual stroke. This putting routine serves the distinct purpose of directing the golfer's attention through a precise sequence of actions that, if followed, heighten concentration and remove distractions by getting the golfer being more there in present time, actually doing these steps instead of having his attention drift off due to a number of interruptions.

When a golfer is suffering from a slump he has most likely dropped out the importance of his intention in the process of hitting putts (or chips) to the hole and he has introverted or fixed his attention on trying to solve the stroke with some kind of mechanical solution or mental idea of blocking out the negative instead of relying on the fundamentals themselves; often his idea of these fundamentals has gone awry.

What I have observed in working with professional tour players and good amateurs on the scoring part of the game is that all good putters had one or more stroke keys. These "keys" combined the mental fundamentals as discussed above and the mechanics of movement.

Successful Putting Keys

Here are some of those "keys" that can help you putt consistently better:

1) Keep the stroke in motion like the flow of a pendulum, going back and through at the same pace.
2) Have a routine that you repeat time after time in the stroke.
3) Get set in a comfortable position over the ball (back off if not ready and start over the putting cycle of action).

4) Lock into a position that holds the body still and allows you to sight the hole and stroke the putt along it.

5) Set up with no tension in the body especially with the shoulders, arms and hands. Keep relaxed, don't tighten the body position, as the body will mirror any mental tension or strain present.

6) Visualize the path of the ball and it going into the cup (repeat this "view" as much as possible with the hands flowing towards the hole along that exact path).

7) Don't think mechanics of the stroke—let your hands get the necessary feel and stroke the putt with the intention of it going in the hole.

8) Rehearse the stroke looking at the hole to groove in the feel and sense of speed.

9) On shorter length putts, listen for the ball at the bottom of the cup (this anchors the head and body position).

10) Be confident and decisive, expect positive results. Reinforce the idea and image of yourself as a good putter, "I'm a good putter," "I'm a great putter."

11) Trust and stroke the putt on the intended line to the hole with confidence. Don't be concerned if in making a good stroke you go by the cup a couple of feet. You'll make more putts if you're striking the putt with authority and decisiveness.

[Note: These are some of the putting keys that great putters use in their games, however not all the steps must be followed].

Putting's Common Denominator

The common denominator to all great putting lies in being *decisive* in the *feel* of the stroke and stroking the putt with the intention of having it go in the hole with no doubts or reservations. Confidence has all to do with certainty and expecting the intended result: The ball going in the cup.

Putting requires the discipline to follow a precise routine that allows for a repeating stroke based on feel that will hold up under pressure.

In order to putt your best, you need to know some "mental keys"[60] to focus on what will produce a well-executed stroke that goes in the cup as planned.

60. mental keys: a chief thought that is used by the golfer on the mental game to execute the swing at is at its highest level of intention. Decisiveness is a good example of a "key."

Over the years I've worked up some drills on putting that have transformed weak putters into excellent ones and good putters into super strokers on the greens. I'll give them to you to use in the next chapter. These drills worked successfully for those on Tour and the scratch amateurs that I have taught. You can work these into a routine that you follow in your practice putting or as a remedy to solve a problem in some aspect of your putting stroke.

Chapter XVI

How to Become a Super Putter in Golf

RULE # 1

In your putting on the practice green and out on the course, you should work towards improving your sense of feel in the stroke with the purpose of making each stroke count and going in the cup.

All good putters work on developing a sense of feel in their stroke. They groove-in a repeating stroke that is both firm and rhythmic and that will stand up under pressure. The sense of feel is crucial and is always senior to the mechanics of the putting stroke itself—so keep this constantly in mind with your stroke.

DRILL #1

Start out a practice or warmup session by stroking a series of long putts in order to determine the feel for the type of greens that you're putting on. The focus here in this stage of practice or before a round is to get a feel for the speed and surface that you're putting on. The training routine here lies in just making a good stroke to the target. Pick a hole or spot some distance away in the twenty to forty foot range and putt to it. Feeling your way with the hands is what you're trying to achieve. The stroke is made without any real conscious effort or thinking. This keeps the stroke from being rigid and mechanical, and allows the stroke to just flow to the hole. Hit putts like this for approximately five to seven minutes or more until you feel that you have achieved a result of the putting stroke feeling comfortable with very little to no tension in the stroke.

DRILL #2

Now concentrate on some shorter mid-range length putts from about fifteen to twenty feet. Stroke these putts to the hole working on the fundamentals in putting: Grip, alignment and rhythmic stroke back and through of the putter head.

The grip should be light, not tight, with the hands working together as a unit. There are many variations of putting grips: Pick the one that feels comfortable in your hands and holds up best under pressure.

The stance, how you set up to the hole, also varies according to what feels right to you and promotes a good hand-eye coordination to the hole. A wider stance is especially good under windy conditions to maintain your balance.

Your alignment should be set with the body (shoulders, hips, and feet) positioned in direct line or slightly open to the hole or in line with the spot where you think the putt will predominantly break, with your eyes over the ball so the stroke can be on line and your eyes follow the path of the ball to the hole.

This quick review of the putting fundamentals gives you the keys to work on in Drill #2.

You should work up the stroke to ensure that your alignment is to the hole from the position you putt from, that your eyes are focused over the ball and in relation to the hole, weight evenly distributed with a little more weight on the left side to anchor the stroke, and that you're working on a smooth back and through motion of the putter to the target that produces a slight end-over-end roll of the putt to cup.

Putting stance to the hole

DRILL #3

This is where you want to work in the mental aspects into your stroke with a pre-putt mental routine. Practicing the stroke a couple of times ahead of time before the actual putt. Many superb putters I have observed will focus directly on the hole itself as if "locking in their scanner" on to the target itself to get the correct read on the putt (the speed and line particularly). They get a feel going in the stroke, then make a decisive stroke back and through to the cup, expecting it to go in.

Looking at the hole in the Rehersal Step (Step 3)

DRILL #4

Spend about five minutes making three-to-five-footers while holding a firm position over the ball during the stroke. Get the back of the left hand and the right working as a unit in the stroke back and through along the intended line to the cup. Place a little more weight on the left side to anchor the body and stroke. Mix in some longer putts to keep the feel going in the stroke and you've got it. End off on a good note that you're confident with your stroke!

This routine of drills (Drill #1, #2, #3, #4) should last any where between fifteen to twenty minutes as a rule but may vary depending on a number of factors for that day's round or practice session.

If you're having trouble with some aspect of the stroke then you need to know how to remedy such a difficulty when it occurs, be it out on the course during competition or during a practice session when you get hung up and it's not working. The next chapter shows you how.

Chapter XVII

Putting Drills and Remedies

These are the particular putting drills that I have found to work for players in the development and improvement of their putting stroke. They can also be used as remedies to get the feel back in the stroke when you're off. Work the following drills into a routine and you'll find yourself a super putter!

DRILL A: LOOK AT THE HOLE DRILL

One of the best remedies that I've employed with my players when they have landed in a slump is "The Look at the Hole Drill."

Purpose: The aim in this drill is to train the hands and mind to work together on "feel" and to stroke the putter without conscious thought or awareness of the stroke. In this training drill you make the stroke while looking at the hole. Thus you take attention off the mechanics of the stroke, and focus more on the hole itself.

Place three or four balls in a row and start making putts to the hole from about fifteen to twenty feet away. Continue making strokes to the cup just working on the timing of the stroke's motion. Really get into a sense of taking the stroke to the hole as the primary objective and entrusting feel to the stroke from what you see as you're looking at the hole.

Emphasis: Importance is placed on developing a sense of rhythm in the stroke and in freeing up one's attention, instead of being fixed more on the stroke and ball itself. This drill develops timing in the stroke and a rhythmic coordination of the hands, arms and fingers to make a smooth, effective stroke to the hole. It puts back that "lost" sense of touch in a stroke that's gotten too rigid and mechanical.

In fact, several pros have putted in such a manner (looking at the hole) in both modern and tournament golf of the late 20s and 30s era. Johnny Miller used it—putting looking at the hole on shorter and mid-range putts the last day or two of the tournament in winning the 1987 AT&T Crosby Pro-Am event at Pebble Beach.

This is an excellent drill for developing feel and rhythm and frees up the stroke and makes it more fluid. It works! You may find yourself thinking of using it. Try it.

End Result: An improved sense of feel and fluidness in the stroke.

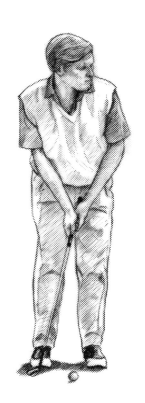

The Look at the Hole Drill

DRILL B: THE ONE HAND PUTTING DRILL

Another good drill is to putt with each hand separately, first with the right hand then with the left, with particular attention to making a complete stroke back and through, guiding the stroke back and through to the hole.

Purpose: To teach the putter to develop feel in the stroke with the one hand that guides and controls the stroke. The golfer will find that in putting one tends to guide and control the putting stroke either with one hand or with both working as a unit.

Emphasis: In this drill the aim is to establish what is working in the stroke, and what hand (if not both), is predominant in making the stroke to the hole. Practice striking a series of putts with each hand, then both, and then back to the hand that seems to get the best roll to the hole. That hand is the one that predominates in your stroke. Pick a distance from about ten to twelve feet to do this. Then use your regular stroke getting the feel of the predominant hand controlling the stroke.

End Result: An improved interaction of the hands, and establishment of which hand action is more dominant in the stroke.

DRILL C: "THE POOL TABLE"/"SLO-MO" PUTTING DRILL

Purpose: This drill is designed to improve your hand-eye coordination and sense of touch in the putting stroke. It's modeled after shooting pool to improve sensitivity and visualization skills, which are so important in the development of the sense of touch in putting.

Emphasis: In this exercise work on "seeing" the break or angle to the hole that the putt must travel on, based on your "read" of the green. Hit a series of putts on a predetermined line to the hole. Pick a series of spots that the path will travel on and visualize connecting them up as the line to the hole—this is what I call the "slo-mo" visualization technique of stringing a line back from and to the target. Work on seeing the line and picking a spot "on the table" to hit your putt to. (This can be used effectively in pitching and chipping as well).

End Result: An improved ability to visualize and pick the line on breaking putts in your putting.

DRILL D: "THE CIRCUIT BREAKER" PUTTING DRILL

Purpose: To rebuild a faulty putting stroke that has become too mechanical, with a better stroke that flows to the hole.

The "Circuit Breaker" is one of my favorite drills. It has worked as a remedy for a number of players.

Emphasis: This drill requires that you *miss* putts to the hole from a short distance of several feet, with emphasis on becoming more creative in purposefully missing putts to the hole on the left and right side, the back corner, etc., to break the negative association of missing a putt and its consequences. Hit putts like this until you feel that you can creatively miss the putt and you find the ball "wanting" to go in instead.

There is a second part of this drill in which the golfer is to putt left-handed if you're right (and vice versa), requiring you to "switch over" to the mirror side of your normal stroke. It gets you to make the stroke newly each time. It creates a new image and impression of the stroke and in doing so cuts directly through the automaticity of your grooved-in "bad" stroke. Your stroke had been developed as a training circuit that you rely on in "muscle memory" or habit, good or bad. By cutting the "automaticity," this drill breaks the circuit and reconstructs a newer spontaneous motion.

End Result: A putter who has grooved-in a better fluid, putting motion and is stroking the putt rather then steering it mechanically to the hole.

DRILL E: THE INTENTION PUTTING DRILL

Purpose: To get the golfer to concentrate on the primary objective of the ball going in the hole and nothing else. It is the intention that dictates the essence or quality of the stroke and is always senior to the stroke (mechanics) itself.

Emphasis: The idea is to train the golfer to look at the putt at hand and "see" the putt going in the cup. Start hitting putts at first to the hole from about five to seven feet. Work on the idea of the ball going in the hole as a direct result of your intention to do so.

Stress the feeling of expecting the putt going in and just doing it. That is the sole criteria. Keep this drill simple. This is not a mechanical drill but a mental exercise. Continue to stroke a number of putts in this manner to where you get an improved felling of confidence and ability to expect the ball going in the hole.

This drill is worked out before the actual stroke in the pre-putt mental routine and is used to peak the intention and decisive execution of the putting stroke. This drill also gives you an idea of what your outlook is and how much attention you place on the mechanics of the stroke.

Hit a series of putts from about 5–7 feet just getting the idea of the ball going into the hole.
The intention of the putt going in is the golfer's primary thought.

The more confident that you are in the stroke, the less attention you have on its mechanics and the more you're focused on the hole and the desire of the intended result, the ball going in. When you have a negative outlook, you'll find yourself being more mechanical as a solution, which is not a solution itself but instead is a problem in your putting.

End Result: A putter who is intent on the putt going in the hole and nothing else.

DRILL F: THE PRE-PUTT MENTAL PUTTING ROUTINE DRILL

Purpose: To incorporate the pre-shot routine into a Pre-putt Mental Routine drill that teaches the correct sequencing of the stroke (surveying, rehearsal, getting decisive, and execution) with particular focus on heightening concentration and mental awareness; in other words, this drill applies the concept of the mental routine to putting.

Emphasis: The stress in this exercise is to follow a consistent routine in one's putting, doing each of the four steps of the pre-putt mental routine completely before going to the next. Start by hitting several putts from a distance of about fifteen feet, going through each step, just as if you were out on the course on the green in an actual putting situation. Work on doing the routine and concentrating on doing each step fully until you feel you are sequencing through without effort and delay in making the stroke to the hole.

End Result: A putter who has a consistent mental routine that works in his putting.

DRILL G: PUTT WITH YOUR EYES CLOSED DRILL

Purpose: Another rather useful exercise especially good on longer putts where there is a problem of not being able to estimate the length and feel of the stroke required is The Putt with Your Eyes Closed Drill.

Emphasis: The training stress is somewhat similar to that of the "Look at the Hole Drill," however in this drill the putter learns to use his "sixth sense" and relies on the feeling of rhythm in the stroke as the guide to feel and speed. This exercise has you hitting putts with your eyes closed and focusing on the "hole over there" instead of the ball. The putter learns that he must focus on both the ball and the hole and see it happening in his mind in making a smooth putting stroke.

You can work this drill into your pre-putt routine rather nicely with emphasis on practicing the putt with your eyes closed or a variation of this in which you make a rehearsal stroke to the hole, and then another practice stroke this time with your eyes closed, yet tuned into a process of seeing the hole and feel of the stroke in your "mind's eye." As a note, this also works nicely in practicing chipping.

End Result: An improved sense of feel, pace, and fluidness in the putting stroke.

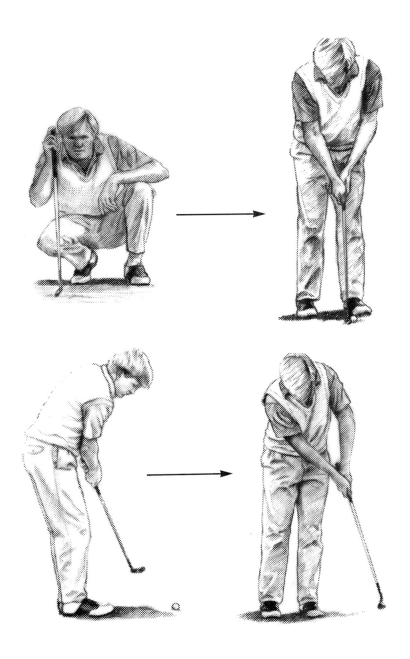

The four steps of the Pre-putt Mental Routine in Putting

Each practice session with putting should culminate with a drill that creates or simulates a competitive environment in order to have some accurate assessment of what kind of feel you have going in your putting. Two drills are suited for this.

DRILL H: "THE BIG THREE OF GOLF" PUTTING DRILL

This drill is often called "The Big Three of Golf Drill" after the "Big Three" or "Triumvirate" of golf in the 60's and 70's: Palmer, Nicklaus and Player.

Purpose: The "Big Three" Putting Drill is a one-on-one putting for honors and lowest score, challenge drill that offers a competitive environment to try out the stroke for "real" in a series of either imaginary simulated matches with the likes of "Palmer," "Nicklaus" and "Player" or going one-on-one with an actual opponent or two for score over nine, eighteen or twenty-seven holes at a time on the putting green. "Carry overs"[61] add more challenge to the match simulating competitive situations and can be your own "Skins Game."[62]

Emphasis: This drill gives you an opportunity to put some heat or pressure on an opponent and try out your stroke and routine in a competitive setting. Work on handling any "buttons" (nervousness) that you may have that cause you to react to the pressure of competition. The best way to do this is by placing yourself in the situation time after time and putting against preferably a real opponent so that competition is not a problem for you but creates an environment that's challenging that will bring out the best in you game.

So if you're having trouble with your short putts, then create competitions on three-to-five foot putts with an opponent or putt long putts that require you to have to make the short ones as a character builder. Actually, your opponent in this drill switches roles, becoming the coach, whereby he helps spot what you're doing that's wrong and points it out to you. You then

61. carry overs: a stroke play situation in which neither of the opponents win the hole, and the prize money is consequently increased or "carried-over" to the next hole of competition, until that hole is won
62 Skins Game: a popular golf game format wherein the golfer who gets the lowest score on the hole and has the most "skins" for the round, wins the competition

apply the advise from the coach. It's best to work on one problem at a time in doing this, if the coach observes more than one outness.

It's important to work through the difficulty that you're having, because if you don't, then that particular area of difficulty will stick your attention or introvert you, and you will have some upset in regards to it. You can minimize or work out the difficulty by continuing to go over the problem, applying the advise of the coach to it. Your instructor makes the best coach in doing this, but don't be afraid to get one of your golf buddies that's a good player to look you over.

End Result: A player who can rise to the occasion and putt well under pressure.

DRILL I: "THE KNEE KNOCKER PUTTING DRILL"

Purpose: To develop confidence in handling the pressure in making the crucial three-to-five foot range putts. These are the putts that make or break a round of golf. A scoring differential of three to eight strokes or more is the result of how well these putts are made.

Emphasis: The importance in this exercise is to train the golfer to hold a position that's rock-steady, keeping the head anchored in the stroke back and through, which when achieved will accelerate the putter on line to the hole. A good tip in being anchored is in "listening" for the ball dropping in the hole before coming up in the stroke.

End Result: A player who is confident and can make short, "knee-knocker" putts at will.

Summary of Putting Drills

Here's a **Summary** of the drills/exercises for you to follow in your practice sessions that will spark super putting success. [Note: You'll most likely find favorites of these drills that you can use more than the others that work in your putting.]

Look At The Hole Drill:
The purpose of this drill is to train the hands and mind to work together on "feel" and to stroke the putter without conscious thought of the mechanics of the stroke. Emphasis here is on developing a sense of rhythm in the stroke and freeing up one's attention with the hole, instead of being fixed on the ball and mechanics. Great drill for developing a better sense of feel in the putting stroke.

What the Other Hand Is Doing Drill:
The purpose of this drill is to determine a proper cause-effect relationship of what each hand is doing in the putting stroke. Emphasis here with this putting exercise is to work out which hand is more dominant, and which one guides the stroke. This will be either the right or left hand, or both. This drill improves the interaction of the hands and establishes which hand is more dominant in the stroke.

The Pool Table Drill:
The purpose of this drill is to improve feel and hand-eye coordination in the putting stroke. Emphasis in this exercise is on getting a "read" for the stroke and visually rehearsing the stroke to the hole, and then executing the stroke to the hole.

"The Circuit Breaker" Drill:
The purpose of this drill is to knock out the automaticity or "circuit" of the mechanics of the stroke. This is where the stroke has become far too rigid and has lost that sense of feel. Emphasis in this exercise is to allow yourself to free up the mechanics of the putting stroke by consciously missing putts, missing four-to-five footers, some on the right side, the left, and at the corners of the hole.

After you feel that you can allow yourself to miss the putt creatively, then work on making a rhythmic fluid stroke without judgment and thinking too much, concentrating on just making the stroke and expecting it to go in the cup.

The Pre-Putt Mental Routine Drill:
The purpose of this drill is to improve the ability to concentrate and bring the stroke to a decisive, well-executed stroke to the hole. The intention and decisiveness are senior to the mechanics of the stroke. Emphasis here is heightening one's focus to make the putt by following an established routine.

Putt With Your Eyes Closed Drill: The purpose of this drill is to improve mental perception and visualization in the putting stroke. Emphasis in this exercise is to duplicate the exact "feel" and its intended line of the putt in the "mind's eye" of the golfer as he makes the putt to the cup.

"The Big Three"/Triumvirate Drill:
The purpose of this drill is to create an actual competitive atmosphere and put your stroke to the test. Emphasis on this exercise is to see just how well you perform under some pressure, taking on a real or imagined opponent and putting eighteen holes or more.

If one has a good pre-putt routine, and can concentrate under pressure and make the stroke with confidence, he will putt well. If not, then continue the above drills until you have mastered them and then try your stroke out again for better success and lower scores in your golf game!

The Knee Knocker Drill:
To train the golfer to make three-footers routinely and increase his confidence on these crucial scoring putts. Emphasis in this exercise is to hold a position with the body that's rock-steady and keep the head anchored and make a confident stroke back and through that hits the ball into the back of the hole.

SUMMARY OF SECTION II: THE MENTAL APPROACH

There is an Inner Game to golf that has to do with the Mental Approach and one's ability to think smart, concentrate, and manage not only the course but oneself in relation to the game. This is the challenge known as the game of golf—the overcoming of barriers and obstacles that the playing field (the golf course) and "Old Man Par" represent in the physical universe and in the universe that we create within ourselves.

Besides learning the rules and the laws that govern the game, the golfer finds that the inherent interest in golf as a game is the overcoming of not unknown barriers: How to hit over water, get out of sand traps, negotiate cutting off a long par four dog-leg hole, etc.. It's the challenges of the game with all the strategy and creative ability required in shot-making that inspire the golfer to rise up and conquer "Old Man Par."

Golf is likely the most difficult and challenging of all games to master. It brings out both the best and the worst in human behavior; the good, bad, and the repulsive in us and in many cases could be best described as a "microcosm of life". Golf may also be the ultimate of all games requiring the utmost skill, intelligence, and resourcefulness of the player to excel at it.

Highlights of the Mental Approach Section

- There is a precise technology to the "Mind Game" that involves natural laws and principles of how the mind works. This part of the game amounts to at least fifty to ninety percent of golf! Without this knowledge, the golfer is adversely affected by his reactions and lacks a true "Ultimate Game of Golf."

- The Inner Game is senior in importance to the Outer Game; what one thinks and considers is always primary in importance to mechanics. The golfer is either thinking causatively, and is positive in his approach, or is being the effect of negative thoughts and considerations that dictate the game. What's in your mind monitors how you function and your results.

- Playing golf is the formulation of thought and its execution into motion in a golf swing. The target provides the action—the motion to be created by the shot maker. The target is the swing's objective.

- PRIMARY LAW IN GOLF: ALL WELL EXECUTED GOLF SHOTS ARE THE RESULT OF BEING DECISIVE AT THE POINT OF HITTING THE BALL TO THE TARGET.

- COROLLARY: ALL POORLY MIS-HIT SHOTS ARE THE RESULT OF BEING INDECISIVE AT THE MOMENT OF EXECUTION.

- Confidence in golf stems from being Decisive, knowing how to play a given shot and expecting the intended result.

- The golfer's intention to make the shot is the chief ingredient in a sound mental approach: The golfer creates the shot, sees it happening, and hits the ball to the target with the idea of it going in or close to the hole.

- The Mind is composed of two parts: the *analytical* and the *reactive* mind. The analytical is that part of the mind that is aware, computes information having to do with solutions and strategies, and involves the creative aspect of shot-making. The reactive part of the mind is a stimulus-response mind that is made up of unpleasant experience, (containing pain or unconsciousness) that when once again encountered or closely approximated in the environment, is restimulated, thus causing an adverse effect on the golfer. Each individual has a number of these restimulators in life that get in the way of their performance.

- The Inner Game of Golf is played in the golfer's mind, in which reactive thought, indecision, and self doubt challenge the analytical mind of the golfer for control over the golfer's actions.

- The Mind is composed of mental image pictures that have recorded in complete detail one's life. All his experience playing golf and sports are recorded in the mind in its various categories that include driving off the tee, fairway shot experiences, putting, up and downs information, types of course played, winning experiences and incidents of losing, type of attitude displayed; it's all filed there as experience both good and bad or later use. (Not only golf and sports; any other incident can be stored too).

- The Mind either works for you or holds you back. One's success potential has all to do with one's desire and intention and the number of restimulators that are adversely affecting the individual in his environment that the golfer/athlete encounters.

215

- The Pre-shot Mental Routine is the technique that integrates the two games of golf into a workable system of execution of the golf shot. It accounts for as much as 50% to 75% of the golf shot. It's the "secret of success" that all good players develop in their game.

- NATURAL LAW IN GOLF: INTENTION IS SENIOR TO MECHANICS. THE QUALITY OF THE GOLF SHOT DEPENDS ON THE AMOUNT OF DECISIVENESS PRESENT AND IS THE DIRECT RESULT OF THE GOLFER'S DEGREE OF INTENTION.

- Attention and Intention are the two chief components that the good player uses in developing a sound mental approach in their game.

- NATURAL LAW IN GOLF: THE TARGET IS THE GOLFER'S PRIMARY FOCAL POINT OF ATTENTION. THE BALL IS THE PRIMARY FOCUS OF MECHANICS. ATTENTION IS SELECTIVELY SHIFTED BACK AND FORTH FROM THE TARGET AS ITS PRIMARY FOCUS AND THE BALL AS ITS SECONDARY FOCAL POINT IN THE PRE-SHOT MENTAL ROUTINE. BOTH BECOME ONE IN FOCUS IN THE EXECUTION OF THE GOLF SHOT.

- Concentration is a key ingredient that combines all three of Golf's Outer, Inner, and Scoring Games for success in one's golf.

- Concentration is actually focusing or shifting of attention onto a specific task or activity. It's doing what you are doing while you're doing it and not off with your attention on something else.

- Leading players describe concentration as a state of mind in which their attention becomes totally absorbed or focused, free from distractions, in hitting the golf ball to the target.

- Winning in Golf is a State of Mind. There is no counter thought or consideration towards the negative, only that of positive intention carried out in its execution of a successful shot. The shot is visualized to go to the target or hole and is carried out in a positive manner, expecting the intended result.

Section III

The Scoring Game

SECTION III

The Scoring Game

The Scoring Game

Chapter I

Becoming a Scoring Threat in Golf

Premise: "The Ultimate Game of Golf" Golfer is not a consummate scoring threat unless he can play the third necessary game in golf—the Scoring Game.

The Scoring Game is that vital part of the game that involves course management and planning. This is the department in which shot-making skill and experience are brought together in a strategic plan of action of how each golf shot will be played. Planning takes into consideration what shots are envisioned, checking against one's strengths and weaknesses and how that action will be executed. This is viewed from the player's inventory of shot-making skills, options, and decisiveness quotient.

The Strategy/Scoring Game is vital to one's mastery of the game. It can make or break a fine performance and score. This is where the real test comes to bear for the golfer, as regardless of his ball striking ability, he must be able to put it all together and become an "Ultimate Game of Golf" Scoring Threat.

In looking over many golf performances with players, there's always a particular pattern that emerges for each player's situation, where he is losing potential shots—areas of his game that he is indecisive and lacking confidence and so forth. So therefore, I've included a chapter here at the beginning of this section in which you can rate yourself on how you're doing on The Strategy/Scoring Section in your game.

Chapter II

Strategy/Scoring Game Questionnaire

1) Do you plan out the hole in front of you in regards to where to place your approach shots?
2) In your golf do you have a strategy that you use to play your best? If so what is it that you do?
3) Do you consider that you have a strength or two in your game that works for you in strategy?
4) Do you find that while playing golf that you are overly swing conscious and think how to make the swing instead of thinking strategy?
5) Do you find yourself playing aggressively, going for the pin or playing too conservatively at the wrong times?
6) Do you have a pattern in starting fast or too conservatively?
7) On the putting green how are you in lagging up[63] your long putts? Consistently long or short?
8) In putting do you tend to go by the cup or to die the putt in the hole?
9) How much do you practice the short game around the greens and work on your putting?
10) Do you change your strategy in a golf tournament from regular course play?
11) Do you play better golf in match[64] play or medal?

If you answered yes on the majority of the questions in the above questionnaire, very good: You are successfully using some form of an effective

---

63. lagging up: getting the approach putt close to the hole
64. match: a form of competition in which the contest is decided hole by hole against an opponent.

223

strategy in your scoring department. If you answered no or sometimes to the majority of the questions, then you are weak in or don't have an effective game plan working in the strategy game needed to be an "Ultimate Game of Golf" Scoring Threat.

You'll score better if you put more attention on strategy and where you can hit the ball, rather than trying to think too much on how you're going to hit your next shot to the target or hole.

Many a golf tournament or match is won or lost where the one golfer outsmarts the other, maneuvering the ball into better position resulting in a higher percentage of shots in play, in the fairway or safely on the green, putting for more pars and birdies than his opponent. The other golfer has not found the groove and is inconsistent, finding himself straining to hit more difficult and aggressive shots to the green in an effort to get back in the match or to even up the score.

Golf is a Game of Strategies and Scoring

Decision-making and course management strategies have to be made in the direction of more correct choices than incorrect ones, in order for the golfer to be a scoring threat. Many golfers fail to recognize the importance of the Strategy/Scoring Game and don't reach their potential even where they have had some success in the Outer Game and Inner Game approaches.

Course management is the combined actions the player takes to be in control of golf's three games. This involves having a handle not only on the mental game and the player's emotions, the swing and its mechanics, but an ongoing process of considering the target and where to place one's shots to it.

Lost too many times in the multitude of thoughts on how to hit the ball (the how to's of mechanics), the golfer fails to actually "see" where to hit the shot on the course in front of him. Instead, the good player is more focused on the target on each shot that's contemplated.

Golf is a game played on an obstacle course of nine or eighteen holes, with a full array of lurking obstacles and barriers, with menacing names like water hazards, bunkers and traps, out of bounds, that lie in wait for the golfer's miscues and errant shots. A golfer gives up a potential four to ten (sometimes more) strokes just in this department alone. If he gave better thought to using some system of strategy as to where to hit the ball on the course, the golfer would play far closer to his potential.

"The Ultimate Game of Golf" Golfer is a scoring threat that is "armed and dangerous," is willing "to fire" on cue to the target. He plots out the correct strategies of when to be aggressive and gamble and where to play more conservative, "percentage" golf shots.

"The Ultimate Game of Golf" Golfer discovers in his own game that the best strategy is the one that uses a game plan[65] to insure success on the course. When it is combined with an efficient swing and a good mental attitude, it will produce better scores.

Golfers' Game Plan

A game plan consists of a series of strategies and tactics that the player will use to defeat an opponent or opposition, namely the likes of "Old Man Par." Such a plan is usually based on the player's resources and strengths.

Game plans differ amongst players and their abilities. The better player will play from his strength working the ball on his tee shots and fairway iron shots either right or left, based on his inclination or tendency to draw or fade the ball. He'll also concentrate his efforts on positioning the ball in that part of the fairway that affords the best angle to work his approach shot to the green or hole.

There is a law in the Scoring Game that has to do with this:

> **ALL GOOD ROUNDS OF GOLF PLAYED ARE THE RESULT OF EFFECTIVE COURSE MANAGEMENT, WELL THOUGHT-OUT GAME PLANS AND DECISIVENESS IN ACTION**

I think that many of us have at one time or another seen the manager of a baseball team swagger up to the pitcher's mound in a tied game situation with bases loaded, to work out the best strategy in facing the opposing line-up of batters. Likewise, in basketball and football games, half-times are essentially times for the coach and players to review team and individual strategies in terms of what's working right or wrong and get regrouped in the effort of winning the game.

65. game plan: a strategic plan of action the golfer uses in his game

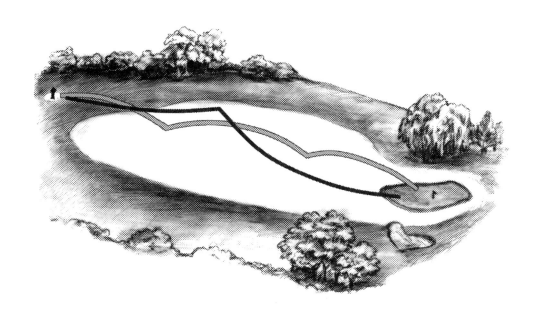

Game Plan and golfer working the ball from right to left

Unfortunately, in golf and other individual sports, this is not the case. The golfer has to rely on himself entirely as the shotmaker and coach, in regards to strategy and "team direction." He has to get up for each shot as his own captain, playing enthusiastically to his highest level of skill and ability. This takes some discipline.

This is a problem for the golfer—having to wear all "hats" at once (player coach, advisor, captain) in a continuous fashion throughout a four and a half to five hour round of golf. This problem is one of the chief reasons why golf is more difficult and more challenging than any other sport. Because of this, apparently good athletes fail to reach their potential at golf, as they were able to do in other less demanding sports.

Strategy is everything in golf competition. An example of this occurred in the 1990 Masters where I had the occasion to observe Greg Norman play the par five fifteenth hole, in which he backed off going for the green on his second shot, going back to the bag, caddy, and yardage card three times in an effort to determine the correct choice of shot (a wood or long iron) to clear the water safely in going for the pin. He then safely hit over the water onto the back part of the green, from where he two putted for his birdie.

How you play the game of golf in overcoming these obstacles makes up your score. The choice of shots and decisions you make, and how well you execute those are the subject of course management and effective strategy in your game.

In golf, it's not always the player with the best-looking swing who is victorious—but is the one who thinks smarter, manages his game better, and sticks closer to a game plan that is built on his strengths—this is what it takes to succeed. It is a game of percentages and near misses, how often you find yourself in the fairway and not in the rough, on the green and not over or in the sand trap, that determines a successful score for the day's round.

All the great players of the game developed their game to a level of proficiency in which they could hit a variety of different shots to the target confidently under pressure.

Being Decisive in Strategy

The key element here, is being decisive in your choice of shots. You'll always hit better, crisper and more solid shots as a result of being sure and decisive.

The legendary golfers of our time knew that there was an "ideal shot" on each shot that was called for, yet they learned from experience that the "correct" shot to hit was not always the one to play, when it came down to getting results. The shot that they felt most confident with was the one they played.

How you manage yourself on the course is of utmost importance. Course management is essential in being an accomplished player. This involves having a handle on not only the mental game, the swing and its shot-making, but on how you stay in control of your emotions, especially in pressure situations. The degree that the player can play and stay focused in his game, and not be affected by past failures and upsetting memories, is what determines success or failure in his game. Many a round of golf has been ruined due to poor leadership on the course.

Let's be realistic in outlook. Golf isn't a fair game. Every golfer can attest to this. Some of your best shots have been penalized by how the ball bounces, having bounced the wrong way at times, costing you a stroke, a scoring opportunity, or a match. Your opponent likewise snakes in a long, downhill putt or chips in from off the green to salvage an "impossible" par. The list goes on and on.

How you react to this, your emotion to it, can either thwart your game, make it worse, or drive you on to excel. "Old Man Par" has a way of beating you, when you least expect it, when you think you've gained that hard won edge, that's the time to beware!

Staying more collected, and not losing your cool or "blowing your top", can save you strokes. As a matter of fact, most of the strokes that you lose to par and your handicap, occur right at the holes in which you "blew up", "lost it," or got real mad. So staying in better control and managing yourself is worth the effort in the scoring game.

As an exercise in course management, you can simply look over your last six scores, and spot the pivotal holes, where you "blew up" or got upset while out on the course. Examine what occurred just before that, that caused this to happen. Evaluate the situation objectively, and learn to catch yourself when reacting, and then shuffle back through your pre-shot mental routine, getting decisive again about the shot you're about to hit.

Remember that realistically, you're going to hit some bad shots that day; its not the end of the world when you do. The good player recognizes this and concentrates on making the next series of shots better. Stay in control of your emotions and play each hole, one by one, as it comes.

GOLF IS A GAME OF STRATEGY IN SCORING

Chapter III

Your Best Strategy is Keeping the Ball in Play

All successful coaches employ a game plan that their team will use in an effort to outscore the opponent. The degree to which they are able to stick to their own plan and throw off the opposition determines the outcome of the game or contest (score) for the winning team.

The good player sizes up the course that he's about to play by knowing where the trouble spots are, what holes are easy and potential birdie and par holes, what shots need to be hit and where not to end up and what to avoid. This is an important and vital step that gives the player a survey of what's to be encountered in playing a particular layout.

Without such knowledge the golfer doesn't know where to direct his plan of action. Just as a boxer "sizes up" his opponent beforehand and during the initial stages of the bout, the experienced player needs to know what he's up against. Then he can be prepared to make better, more intelligent choices in his shot-making.

The good player may well practice various shots that are called for on this particular course layout during a practice round, in preparation of a second encounter or upcoming tournament, paying particular attention to such factors as how wide are the fairways for the tee shot, is the landing area tight and narrow, what kind of trouble is there on this course (water, sand and out of bounds), the type and speed of the greens, prevalent wind conditions, where not to drive off the tee or go over the green, where to lay up[66] and not gamble a shot.

66. lay up: a strategy in which the golfer hits his approach shot short of the target or green in an effort to capitalize on a better position to hit the next shot to the hole

Good players may work on perfecting their long irons more in order to reach the long par fours or in laying the ball up from off the tee on a tight narrow par four hole. They may put some extra time in their practice session on "feathering"[67] their wedge shot from forty yards and closer with courses that have more demanding greens conditions. They may work on the sand shot from semi-buried and buried lies or the finesse shot from tall grass around the greens.

Golfers' Strengths

All golfers have a strength, something that they do better than other parts of their game. Many golfers tend to overlook this and find fault with their entire game and end up being too critical of themselves. Their game becomes a generalization of all being bad, instead of validating some of the good.

If your inclination is to hook or draw[67] the ball to the target as a pattern in your shot-making then this is your basic (game) plan with which you're going to set up your shots to play the course in front of you. This plan is what gives the golfer a sense of controlling his shots that he can hit in a certain way to the target. The game plan is discussed in more detail in the next chapter.

If your chipping is strong or you drive long and relatively straight, then this is an area of your game that's getting you results. The more areas of your game that you are confident with, the better you'll play. So a good game plan will call for using these strengths often. The best pros are strong in every aspect of the game, in the long game and the short; they do it all quite well. Nick Faldo, Tom Kite and Curtis Strange are a good example of this.

The areas that you have the most trouble with will be where you lose more strokes to par or your handicap than you should. These are potential strokes lost instead of gained. So any efficient strategy that you use on the course must be formulated around those areas in your game that you do better than the rest.

This reminds me of the game that I witnessed as a teenager in Chicago at the North Shore Country Club in Glenview, Illinois, where my grandfather

67. feathering: the art of hitting finesse shots in shot-making. Examples would be a punch or knock down shot, the cut or lob shot with the wedge
68. draw: a slight hook in which the ball goes from right to left

230

shot an 80 on his eightieth birthday and was carried off the course by his playing partners—a difficult course that has hosted a U.S. Open and Amateur tournaments.

Not long but deadly straight, my grandfather would get drives out about 170–180 yards and would fire his trusty 4 wood another 160–170 yards with its roll. He was a good chipper and a very good putter with his old wooden shaft, mallet putter and put it all together on that momentous occasion.

So you see, it can be done. Playing one's best shots, hitting the "percentage shots," and keeping the ball in play, is more consistent than going for the very risky, untried shots, which may very well go out of bounds or land in a water hazard, etc..

Accuracy pays off dividends and smart approach shots reap better scores in the form of pars and birdies—the same strategy worked for me as a kid at age ten as a junior champion, breaking 80 with straight, though not long drives and a lot of deft chips and one-putts to my credit! Many a major golf tournament has been won by eighteen pars on the final day such as Nick Faldo's 1986 British Open victory at Murfield.

The Scoring Game

Chapter IV

Developing a Game Plan in Your Golf

A golfer has to wear a number of hats in order to play his best. There's of course, the player's hat of hitting the shots, and that of being in control of one's mental approach, and lastly, but not the least important, the role as the strategist in the scoring game. The player must have a solid foundation in The Outer and Inner Game approaches in order to be able to score well with The Strategy Game.

Rule in Golf

The golf course determines the type of shot you play. Scoring has all to do with how you play the course in front of you. Your overall goal as a player besides producing the best possible score against "Old Man Par," is to advance the ball in a step by step progression, from tee shot to approach shot, to short shots around the green, and finally to putts in the hole. It's important to your strategy to pick a specific target for each shot you play. Target focus is the name of the game when it comes to strategy. Remember, that in the final analysis of your round of golf, it's only the score that counts, nothing else. A golfer doesn't get points for his swing's form. Everyone seems to have just one question about your round of golf and that is, "what did you shoot today?"

In order to be a scoring threat you need to have a game plan that's molded around your game. Your game consists of a series of areas: strengths and weaknesses that come into play. The best game plan is to pay more attention

The good player sizes up the course, where the trouble spots are, what shots need to be hit,
and surveys what's to be encountered

to and play your own game, because that's the one that you're most familiar with. No one knows your game better than you, except perhaps your instructor. In sports, professional coaches are hired to bring out the best of the teams' strengths and eliminate weaknesses in the lineup. They know that successful performances are the result of utilizing their strengths and sticking to that which works time after time. They can beat the opponent more times than not if they stick to their game plan. The same applies in golf.

As a golfer this means hitting shots that you feel confident about—shots that you have a degree of control or consistency with. You have a working idea what these are. By playing these shots, you not only keep the ball in play more often, but lessen the chances of having to hit shots that you're unfamiliar with; thus you're scoring potential and its outcome will be better.

Be realistic. Don't hit shots that you can't really hit or think you should be hitting. You might envision the correct shot that a pro would hit in a given situation, but remember that you're not Arnold Palmer or Jack Nicklaus and even then there is more than one way to play a given shot, so play the one that you feel is more of the percentage shot that keeps the ball in play, not over in the bushes or trees in the rough.

Here's a drill that can be done in practice that will help with this. This drill works best on the course (where permitting) or can be done in a limited manner at the range depending on what kind of targets and greens are available to hit to.

HITTING FROM YOUR STRENGTHS DRILL

Purpose: To teach the golfer to recognize the importance of playing golf from his strengths—those areas in his game that he has confidence in and can get results with.

It's an invariable rule that the golfer will always play better by playing from his strengths. Strengths become game plans. Although golfers need to improve their weak areas in their game, they will find that where they validate the good areas (I'm good off the tee, great with the putter, etc.) they play better golf.

Emphasis: The training stress is placed on learning to hit the shot that the golfer considers will get him the best result; this may well mean that he allows for a draw or fade[69] and play from that tendency in his shot-making, pitch and run his longer chip shots instead of trying to finesse the wedge which would be more difficult for him. The golfer needs to avail himself of smart shots that will cause a higher percentage of opportunities based on what he can do instead of what he hopes will happen.

This drill is to be done ideally out on the course in a practice session, in which the golfer plays four to six holes of golf with two or three balls going, selecting different shots to hit in his strategy (strength, semi-strength, weakness). He is to note how he does when he plays from his strengths, and from the other choices that he played. Doing this drill can also help establish what your strengths are in your golf as well.

End Result: A golfer who knows what his strengths are and can use them in a game plan that produces better results.

69. fade: slight left to right curve or slice

235

Chapter V

Thinking Smart is the Name of Golf's Scoring Game

Too many golfers fail to reach their potential mainly due to thinking during the wrong time with the shot—trying to figure out how to make the right swing over the ball—instead of work out the particulars ahead of time. The thinking mode takes place before the swing in the pre-shot routine. This is evident in the mental routines of good players of the game.

That's why a Pre-shot Routine is important. The golfer follows a precise sequence of actions that he performs, based on experience, creative imagination, and the employment of his game plan of strengths (confidences) and weaknesses as discussed earlier in this section.

Thinking smarter, saving strokes, and playing for score on the course is an entirely different matter from what occurs on the range. It requires a different approach if you're going to master the scoring part of your game.

This part of the golf game has been neglected in golf instruction, which, as we discussed in Part I of *The Ultimate Game of Golf,* has emphasized 90–95% on swing mechanics. Golf needs to be taught more out on the course.

Players will benefit from lower scores when they balance instruction on swing mechanics with playing lessons on the course with an instructor or good player. The reason for this is that seeing how a professional plays the course and their particular approach in hitting shots in different actual situations can give you key insights into strategy and in selecting more appropriate shots to hit.

This gives you the benefit of thinking more decisively with your own game. From such a playing lesson you can see where your game is breaking down, lacking confidence, and is costing you strokes and from which you can start tackling your weak areas to improve.

Good players are thinking about position on the shot and set up the hole based on where they envision they should be so that they can hit their "bread and butter shot" (their best, most reliable shot), to the pin in order to make a birdie putt. In other words, they're thinking ahead...somewhat like a good chess player or field general must do.

Chapter VI

Some Key Points in the Strategy/Scoring Game

There are several key points in the strategy game to keep in mind in scoring your best. Let's examine each of these points.

Tee Shot

This is your offensive weapon in "The Ultimate Game of Golf" arsenal. The old maxim, "Drive for show, putt for dough" rings true...but lets flank it with this advise: "Drive for length but do not sacrifice position." Go with the tee shot that you can land in the fairway the majority of times. If the driver isn't working, then tee off with the three wood or a two or three iron.

Play more aggressively on the holes that are wide open. Use the driver in these situations, especially on par fives that are wide open off the tee and bust it! Go with the wood or driving iron that's getting results.... Don't deviate in strategy off the tee, unless you're confident and even so hit for position.

Choose a layup shot with a three or four wood, or three iron on a tight par four hole where accuracy and position reward the player's second shot to the green. Remember: there's no premium in going for broke with the driver off the tee where the fairway is narrow (unless when you really need to, say even the match or makeup several strokes with a couple of remaining holes in stroke play). Hitting the ball in the rough or behind a tree not only takes you out of position to the green, but can lead to another bad shot if you gamble and ends up costing you strokes.

Fairway Shot

Hit your fairway shot to the green using enough club, not having to press with a big swing where you are apt to lose your balance and control and come-over[70] the shot. If you can't reach the green in two, then hit a four or five wood, or a long iron in position just in front or around the green. From here you can chip onto the putting surface and still make your par. Emphasis on the fairway shot is in making solid contact with the ball.

Getting Up and Down[71]

Your strategy in this department is to go with the percentage shot—the pitch or chip with the least lofted club. There are exceptions to this, but the rule of thumb is to let the ball roll more to the hole where there's room. This is because there's more control on such a shot than trying to land the ball closer to the hole, which can be harder to do especially in pressure situations.

Choose anywhere between a five to eight iron for this purpose. Pick out a spot approximately one-third the distance from the hole and make that where you're going to land the ball. Get the ball going to that spot. The ball will then run the remaining distance to the hole depending on your choice of iron. Go with the wedge when you need to loft or finesse the ball to a tight pin position.

Getting up and down from a sand shot depends chiefly on the type of lie in the trap and the distance to the pin. Set up with the shoulders, hips and feet open or left of the hole with the face of the wedge open to the target and "spank" the ball out of the sand towards the hole!

Such alignment promotes a steep takeaway going back, and an outside-in motion which explodes the ball out of the sand. The objective is to get out of the bunker and close enough to the hole from where you can have a run at a makeable putt and salvage your par. This isn't a difficult shot to hit if you'll just practice it and get some familiarity with its different situations.

Putting from off the green can also be an effective stroke-saver in the getting up and down department. Use the "Texas wedge"[72] where there's a short fringe and you can putt the ball instead of chipping it. This shot is a

70. come-over: the action of the golfer's right shoulder hitting too quickly or
    crossing over in the forward swing to the target
71. getting up and down: a chip, pitch or sand shot in which the player gets the ball on
    the green and makes his putt usually to save par

240

Green

The golfer putting from off the green

judgment call that depends on the circumstance and your preference.

Putting on the Green

Strategy in putting is as simple as this: Get all your approach putts close to the cup. On long putts this should be within three feet. You will then hole the majority of those putts on a routine basis. Envision a three foot circumference around the hole. Aim to have the putt end up in this circle or "basket."

72. Texas wedge: a specialty shot in which the golfer uses a putter off of the green instead of chipping, where the surface is flat in front of the green and the hole

On all other putts from about twenty-five feet or closer you should be thinking only one thought: Making the putt! A good strategy on ten footers and closer is to not come up in the stroke, but "listen" for it dropping in, and stroke the putt firm enough so that it goes about a foot and a half by the hole if you do miss it.

The reason for this is that a firmer stroke will keep the putt more on the line and hole more putts percentage-wise. There are however, great putters of the game who died their putts in the front of the hole; Bobby Jones was one of these.

Remember, as we discussed in Part II on The Mental Approach to Golf, the importance of coming to a decision point on each shot and carrying it out in hitting your shot; that's what we're looking for here. You can't be thinking mechanics when you need to be focused on strategy.

If you're not sure about the shot or some aspect of it, then elect something about the shot that you can do—advance the ball closer to the green or closer to an area of fairway where you want to, but make the shot count in setting up an easier, more confident shot in position for the next one. On days where you're feeling more confident and in control of your game, you can play more aggressively to the target or hole, where you are causing opportunities to come about for better scores.

Hit those shots you feel you can hit, play more aggressively on shots that you're confident with and you'll find this to be a workable formula to use in your game for score on the course.

Many golfers get so engrossed with trying to figure out the swing while out on the course that they tend to "forget" the strategy game. It's a good idea to keep in perspective that golf is a game played on an obstacle course of no less than nine holes and that each of these holes is designed around a certain degree of difficulty. Your strengths act as a guideline for you to play the hole.

Another method is to consider looking at the eighteen holes that you are about to play in sets of three, with six holes in each set, consisting of the opening six holes, the middle six and the closing six holes. For example, let's say you play the open six holes great or you find that you get off to a poor start. You can then change your strategy on how you are doing in relationship to this and make any necessary changes (such as playing more aggressively or more conservatively).

It's important for you to get off to a good start and establish a sense of timing in your swing to increase your confidence a little more. Play conservatively at the start over the first series of holes (unless your pattern is to open fast and has been successful). Depending on how you are doing, you can adjust your strategy based on the results you're getting. The idea is to build upon your confidences, set a rhythm, get into a pre-shot mental routine and play the course as each hole unfolds before you.

When you find yourself playing poorly and "groping for a better swing," go back to a quick review of fundamentals, especially the triangle relationship of Timing (Balance, Tempo, Rhythm), check grip (arms too tight or loose), and alignment position. A better sense of timing in making a smoother-paced, controlled swing to the target in many cases can handle the problem on the spot.

The Scoring Game

I have put together a series of drills that can help you play better and become an "Ultimate Game of Golf" Scoring Threat. They are to be done in the order that they appear. After you have gotten to know them, you can drill the later, more comprehensive ones (4–11). These drills are basic to the fundamentals of an effective golf strategy and need to be periodically reviewed and done. Any particular drill can act as a remedy as well.

Chapter VII

Strategy and Scoring Game Drills for Section III

1) LOCATING THE TARGET/HOLE DRILL

Purpose: To teach the golfer to spot where the green or hole (target) is in relation to where he is on the tee, in the fairway, or at greenside. Many times the golfer becomes so engrossed in the mechanics of the swing that he doesn't really focus his full attention on the target and on a strategy of what to do with the golf shot at hand.

Emphasis: This is a simple drill that requires directing one's attention onto the target or hole for consideration of the right choice of shots to hit, which is the initial sequence of the pre-shot routine. This initial read of the shot to be played is all important.

The golfer should spend more time in the selection of the correct shot to hit and in a quick rehearsal of the swing itself (if needed), than in thinking mechanics over the ball. This drill works best where the player can be out on the course, when the course is not busy and can hit extra shots to the target.

End Result: A golfer, who in his strategy can sight the target or hole and can select a correct shot to hit.

2) SETTING UP THE HOLE AND SHOT DRILL

Purpose: To train the golfer to plan out how to play a given golf hole or shot and decide on the best shot-making strategy to use to obtain the desired results.

Emphasis: In this drill the player focuses on the layout or hole itself that he is playing, actually "seeing" the hole and where the tee shot or fairway shot should end up to the target, giving him the best possible approach to the fairway or green. Each hole has a feel about how it can be played. The player learns to respond to the requirements of the hole in front of him.

He does this first by going over to the side of the tee nearest the hole lay-out post, (which graphically shows the outline of the hole, its yardage and handicap) and gathers information from it. He can also confer with his scorecard, and his yardage notes as well in assessing the scene. He then moves closer to the middle of the tee for observation.

He observes what is obvious about the hole: The contour of the hole, how narrow is the landing area, the best angle to the green for the second shot, where there is any trouble that comes into play (fairway traps, water hazards, rough or mounds). He quickly gathers all his data and plans on how he's going to play the hole. He now decides on the correct shot to hit.

In doing so the golfer should realize that it's the decision or plan that's important on where he's going to hit the tee shot that's important in this drill. Particular attention to the planning step (Step 2—Decide) of the pre-shot routine should be made, resulting in the selection of a shot that he can hit with some degree of confidence.

End Result: A golfer who can confidently set up to play a given golf hole or shot in a workable strategy.

3) STICKING TO YOUR GAME PLAN DRILL

Purpose: To teach the golfer the importance of sticking to a game plan, using a strength, and where to direct his shots to the target; in other words, thinking strategy on each shot to hit.

Emphasis: The golfer is to walk up to the middle of the tee and determine, after he has all pertinent information about it, how he's going to play the hole in front of him. He is to adopt a plan, (Step 2: Decide from the Pre-shot Routine) to play the type of tee shot that he feels he can hit the fairway with, his strength (be it hitting it straight, draw or fade).

He's to next line up the shot so that he utilizes the best angle of the fairway to drive the ball to. He's to then hit decisively to that position. The golfer is to follow the same routine for the second shot in the fairway, and in his approach shots to the green.

Particular attention on recognizing the player's strengths and playing from a game plan in his strategy is emphasized. The golfer must realize that play on the golf course is for score only and playing from a plan is the chief component of effective strategy. Playing from a game plan is what gets decisive results in a golfer's game.

End Result: A golfer who can recognize and play from his game plan and applies smart strategy on the golf course resulting in improved performance.

4) THE TWO BALL STRATEGY DRILL

Purpose: To help establish patterns of strengths from what's working for the player and further his game plan that will result in more effective strategy and results in scoring.

Emphasis: In this drill the golfer is to play two balls on each shot. He is to elect to play each set in a particular way, say more conservatively with ball A, and more aggressively with ball B. The totals are compared at the end of each hole and round. The ball with the lowest combined score wins a point. This winning combination is the game plan that the player then uses in a systematic, objective approach in his scoring game.

End Result: A golfer who confidently knows his game plan works and produces better scores.

5) BEING DECISIVE IN YOUR SHOT-MAKING STRATEGY DRILL

Purpose: To train the golfer on the importance of following through on a decision in shot-making strategy and not getting hung up on what to do on the given shot.

Emphasis: In this drill it's important for the golfer to complete the survey step (Step I) of the pre-shot mental routine; sizing up the shot at hand and being decisive (Step II) about his choice of shots. His final choice should be consistent with his overall shot-making strategy which uses his strengths as a guideline. Indecisiveness is the major source of error in shot-making miscues.

This drill is done out on the course where the golfer has to decide which shot to hit. Start with hitting from off the tee to get a feel for where you're going to place the drive and then work in closer to the target, paying particular attention to making decisions and selecting particular choices. Find your strength in your shot-making, then make shots that use that strength. Practice on this drill will help reduce the amount of indecision in shot-making and will improve overall score.

End Result: A golfer who can be more decisive in choosing the correct shot to hit in his shot-making strategy, and can use that strategy as an advantage.

6) KEEPING THE BALL IN PLAY DRILL

Purpose: To show the golfer that by keeping the ball in play better he can create more opportunities to score in his game.

Emphasis: This is a strategy drill that is done in a practice session on the course. The golfer is to hit more than one ball off the tee (where permitted) and hit the following shots: 1) a regular smooth swinging drive for placement, 2) an aggressive decisive, "go for it drive," 3) a conservative drive or three wood lay up shot. This can also be done on the second shot in the fairway shot as well.

The golfer is to assess the results of the above exercise and to note what each type of shot making produced. It will be found that the golfer who keeps the ball in play longer, hitting the percentage shot throughout a round of golf creates more opportunities to score, being in better position to do so.

The majority of errant golf shots in the strategy game are the result of indecision over the correct shot to hit due to not making up one's mind. There is a time to play aggressively and gamble on a golf shot, and times to play conservatively, in one's strategy.

The trick is to know when to do so and you cannot go wrong by playing and sticking to your game plan. If you don't have a game plan then adopt one!

End Result: A golfer who by keeping the ball consistently in play creates scoring opportunities.

7) WHEN TO CHANGE YOUR STRATEGY DRILL

Purpose: To know when you need to change strategies during a round of golf.

The golfer may find himself confronted with a situation in which his game plan isn't working that day or during a longer stretch of play, say at a golf tournament. His game plan consists of playing from his strengths to get the best possible score; these strengths may be one or more in his game, such as driving long and straight, getting the ball up and down and putting well.

The golfer in this drill has to learn when to "shift gears" and change his current strategy to something else, when the situation warrants it.

There are a number of situations in which you'll need to change strategies: 1) when the driver is consistently getting you in trouble, 2) when your putting has gone to hell and you can't seem to make anything in sight, 3) when you can't "hit the barn" even if your life depended on it with your short irons from 120 yards or less, and 4) when you just can't seem to make things go right despite anything in your game.

These situations do realistically occur to a golfer and he'll need to deal with them accordingly as "the game must go on." I recall an article in the sports section of Los Angeles Times several years ago, during one of the LA Open golf tournaments in which Tour player Mark O'Meara made the comment that there were only a handful of days during a given month out on Tour in which his game was at its best, both physically and mentally.

Here's two drills that apply to when you need to change your strategy.

8) "WHEN NOTHING'S GOING RIGHT" DRILL

Purpose: To get "the wheels back on" and "to recover quickly." In situations when it "ain't all falling into place," the golfer needs to go to his fundamentals and review what produces a good shot and come to some rather prompt conclusion of what's wrong with the current scene.

Emphasis: The golfer in this drill has to learn when to "shift gears" and change his current strategy to that of something else when the situation warrants it.

This is done by doing one of the remedy drills from The Outer Game Section such as the Step Back/Step Through, Swing Lever, and/or The Takeaway Drill; one of these drills may well start to handle the scene right away or improve the scene little by little.

This drill has to do with getting into motion with the swing and is a good remedy in itself for that particular reason, as in many cases golfers are playing poorly due too much thinking over the ball, getting too serious, which adds up to poor concentration. This violates the pre-shot mental routine; in any case the thing to do here is to get the golfer to regroup with the fundamentals, play more conservatively, and regain his confidence and composure.

There's a mental component to this as well here and this can be remedied in a lot of cases by a quick review of the mental fundamentals (from The Inner Game/Mental Approach section of this book) especially the drill, Being Decisive and the Pre-shot Mental Routine Drill. Slowing down one's breathing and getting a rhythm reestablished are of prime importance in the use of remedies that can get the golfer along with the above drills back on track in one's game.

There's another situation in which the golfer needs to change his strategy, and that's when the golfer is on a roll and playing confidently.

9) WHEN IT'S GOING RIGHT AND YOU'RE SCORING WELL DRILL

Purpose: To learn to stick to that which is producing results and not change one's strategy when playing your best golf. In this situation the golfer is in a higher state of mind and ability that he can play more aggressive and "fire on cue" to the target and hole with authority and confidence. Some players refer to this state as "being in the zone."

Emphasis: As a training drill the golfer will find that when he is experiencing such a state of mind, and playing above his potential, that he will be very buoyant emotionally, and will be "pumped up" physically. He's being very decisive in his shot-making, and his strategy is more directed towards firing his shots aggressively to the pin. He has most likely hit several career shots in his round of golf, and holed a number of putts.

He has experienced to some degree a "close encounter of the golf kind," and is in a spirit of play concerning his game. When this is happening, the golfer is to go with the flow, not think about how he's doing, and keep doing what he's doing that's producing such results.

This drill can be done out on the course or in a field, playing against an opponent or imaginary one, such as a Jack Nicklaus or Greg Norman or some other favorite player. This can be done on each shot, or on an iron shot or on an up and down situation, or at any time by throwing down a ball and "taking on your opponent."

The player drills this situation in the following way. He works on getting himself totally positive about the results of the shots he's about to hit. His strategy is to play aggressively and fire the ball to the target, or landing area in the fairway off his drive, with no thought of any negative consequence.

The idea is to get yourself psyched up, and create an atmosphere of confidence. Work on challenging your opponent and hitting decisive shots to the target. [This is a fun drill that I did a lot as a junior golfer when I practiced, as we couldn't always play when we wanted].

End Result: A golfer who knows in his strategy what to do when he encounters playing and scoring well.

10) HANDLING STRESS AND INDECISION IN STRATEGY DRILL

Purpose: To train the player in how to deal with stress and indecision when they interfere with the golfer's strategy in shot-making.

Emphasis: How one deals with stress and indecision can make or break a golfer's game. This is a real problem that keeps a number of golfers from achieving their goals; they really don't have a game plan or strategy to deal with and handle the effects of stress and indecision.

In this drill the golfer gets his instructor or a close golfing associate to go out on the course with him and play against him. The instructor or golfing buddy is to select a couple of "areas" that the player has trouble with: the "stuff" that he reacts to, especially having to do with shot-making and its strategy. The player is to go about his shots not knowing when the instructor golfing friend is going to interject one of these "areas" or remarks about the choice of shots that the golfer selects in his shot-making task.

The golfer is to sequence through his pre-shot routine not reacting to the suggestions and comments made by his counterpart as they play competitively a round of golf. The instructor/golf buddy comments are aimed at trying to throw the player off and invite the player to be distracted and thus abandon his game plan as they continue play. The drill is kept going if the golfer continues to react to the baiting. When he is able to concentrate and play undistracted by such distractions the player has accomplished the purpose of the drill.

End Result: A golfer who can handle stress and indecision in his Strategy/Scoring game.

An additional drill that the golfer can do as part of the above drill is the "Practice Backing Off The Shot" Drill. This is for those situations in which the player senses indecision and pressure and must back off the shot, otherwise face hitting a potentially bad golf shot.

11) PRACTICING BACKING OFF THE SHOT STRATEGY DRILL

Purpose: To train the player in how to deal with stress and indecision when they interfere with the golfer's strategy in shot-making.

Emphasis: In this drill the player learns that there will be times when he's indecisive about a particular golf shot that he's about to play. There will be something about the shot that he is uncertain about, that's hanging him up. This could be something like being in between clubs and not sure which to hit, being distracted by others in his group or on the course, thinking about some off the course problem or matter, still upset about the previous hole, etc..

The player is to not hit the shot, but is to back off and regather his thoughts and go through his pre-shot mental routine again. He is to then treat this shot like he's looking at the shot for the first time, and is to make sure that he's decisive about it. He is to then fire the shot to the intended target with confidence.

This drill is an exercise in getting one concentrating so that the proper strategy can work for the player. It can be done out on the course or at the range as well.

A number of touring pros do this. They get their concentration back in when they are ready to hit the shot to the target and turn stress around to their advantage; Billy Casper is a good example of such a player, who would stop, back-off the shot, and put the club back in his golf bag. He would then go through the whole routine once again as if he was hitting the shot for the first time.

End Result: A golfer who can back off a shot, get refocused and decisive, and keep his strategy working in his shot-making.

Chapter VIII

Summary of the Strategy and Scoring Game Section III

- "The Ultimate Game of Golf" Golfer is a scoring threat, who can think smart on the course, use his strengths, and create scoring opportunities and can thus get the most out of his game.

- LAW IN GOLF: ALL GOOD ROUNDS OF GOLF AND THEIR PERFORMANCES ARE THE RESULT OF WELL THOUGHT-OUT, DECISIVE GOLF SHOTS BASED ON CHOICES OF STRENGTHS IN SHOT-MAKING.

- Golf is a Game of Strategies in Scoring. All decision-making has to be made in the direction of scoring and in making more right decisions than incorrect ones.

- The key element in selecting the right shot is being decisive and going with the club that you can hit with some degree of confidence and control.

- The Strategy/Scoring Game is a formula of hitting the correct percentage shots, knowing when to be aggressive, and when to play more conservatively.

- "The Ultimate Game of Golf" Golfer discovers the importance of a game plan and in sticking to it. The degree to which the golfer can adhere to that plan determines his success in golf.

- The good golfer surveys and sizes up his opponent, "Old Man Par," where the trouble lies and where to direct his game plan of strategies.

- Play your own game, make your own decisions, stick to your strengths and game plan: this is your formula for the Strategy/Scoring Game.

- You'll play better golf and score better if you put more attention on strategy as to where you hit the ball rather than trying to think too much on how you're going to hit your next shot.

- All in all, go with the shots that are producing results in your long and short game: These are usually your strengths. Go with these when thinking strategy and scoring.

- Play more aggressively on shots when your confidence is up, and when the situation warrants it. You can "open up" on holes that are more open and go for the big drive, second shot, or putt.

- The idea is to build upon your confidence. Get a rhythm going in your swing. Use your pre-shot routine and use an effective strategy that will play the course in front of you in the least of amount of strokes.

- When playing poorly, check for thinking too much on the mechanics of the swing, instead of where you're going to place the next shot. Quickly review your fundamentals: Alignment and grip, timing, pre-shot mental routine, and game plan strategy.

- Play the course in front of you, play each shot and hole with a plan in mind and play your own game!

How To Play To Win Section

There is a winning philosophy that "The Ultimate Game of Golf" Golfer needs to have in order to win at golf that I want to cover here.

First of all, being armed with and knowing the data that works and produces results in your game is not enough. "The Ultimate Game of Golf" Golfer needs to constantly be improving his skill and applying the data from this book and those mentioned herewithin. There is some excellent material and information in these sources that I have listed that will further your knowledge of this great game. I encourage their reading and study. Competence is demonstrated when you can produce the necessary shots that need be mastered under the utmost situations.

Golf is essentially a game of wins and losses; in a sense is a game of the management of the near misses. In golf there isn't an absolute that's attainable—only to reach the level of potential and skill that you can is the aim. The ultimate test is to the degree to which you attain that objective.

Golf's Primary Goal: Enjoyment

The golfer that succeeds is the one, who despite the set backs, doesn't get stuck in losses, and is the one who thinks that he can achieve worthwhile goals and does. That individual is committed to the game and what it takes to play the best that he can, and persists in doing so.

Along with this, the good players of the game are truly being professional in outlook and develop an attitude that golf is a great game that provides an environment to set challenging goals to reach toward.

It's important to develop the frame of mind, regardless of being an amateur or pro, to do what you do as a professional and continue to work up to the highest standard that you can achieve. A professional viewpoint involves making intelligent choices and accurate assessments of one's strengths and weaknesses as one goes, and overcoming the barriers and stops that get in the way to one's progress.

Mental Attitude

Winning in golf has more to do with your attitude than with any other factor. Its not all the tournaments that get won, as every time one wins someone has to lose, but has to do with how you play the game, uphold your personal integrity, and how you respect the rules and treat your opponents—that's of paramount importance and is what really counts when you get down to it.

Overcoming the barriers and obstacles that get in the way and reaching your objectives is the satisfaction of being as professional as you can be at your level of play.

The biggest difficulty that the golfer has to deal with during a round of golf is staying in control when he is hitting poor, bad shots that lead to the "wheels coming off." Most golfer miscues, lack of concentration, and errant golf shots are the result of a series of bad shots and/or holes which upset the player and produce certain mental phenomena that trigger further upset and turmoil.

One develops set attitudes in regards to the various parts of one's game. For example, if you chronically putt poorly, then you find yourself dealing with a set of mixed reactions or feelings that are negative in expression in regards to your scoring game. If your sand shot is terrible or you just can't chip then the negative part of your mind "seeks air time" and reinforces this losing image of yourself as a bad putter or chipper.

Accompanied with this are negative, reactive phrases or dialogue that take control of the golfer, and thus render him ineffective analytically. These attitudes are fixed ways that players respond to those particular aspects of their games and will "see" their games through a preconceived fabric or through colored glasses.

Many golfers fear the idea of hitting a bad shot, thinking that once done, this will cause a rush of additional bad shots to happen, and before the player knows it another bad golf shot has been reeled off. This can at times get so bad that golfers can predict that this phenomenon will occur especially when they have a good round of golf going and they have exceeded their "comfort zone," and don't want to blow it, and make more mistakes. The more they resist and try to prevent this from happening, the more their attention becomes fixed on trying at all costs to avoid a bad shot, and consequently this is exactly what happens after all.

Trying to block out the negative actually brings more attention to it. What you picture you perceive as "real." What you need to do is forget about the consequences of a bad shot and its penalties and think more on the outcome of what could positively happen and be able to accept and have a bad shot if you hit one for what it is, a miscalculated shot, nothing more.

It's best to face or confront the situation and be analytical about what's happened, be realistic about your shot-making, that you are going to make some bad shots for whatever reason, and that every time that you actually play you're going to hit some bad ones and come back with good ones as well. This is not easy to do and to master. You've got to trust your perceptions and sense of feel and keep these factors working in your game.

All errant golf shots are the result of being indecisive about the shot at hand; a breakdown in concentration, nothing more than that.

Bobby Jones knew the importance of concentration in the golf swing, but could predict realistically hitting four or five bad shots a round each time he teed up to play. He accepted this and would not let it destroy his game, but also knew that he would hit some good shots that would average out the bad. The rest were average that are part of the eighteen hole package.

I think that there is a prevalent myth that the touring pro hits the ball perfectly all the time, which is not true. They hit bad shots and get the ball out of position too, but have the ability to come back with a good shot, and get the ball up and down with authority and confidence. A bad shot gets their necessity levels[73] up, "their blood running," and concentration back in a hurry.

What It Takes To Win

What makes golf such a challenge and a difficult game to master is the fact that it's you and no one else who's out on the course, going head to head with "Old Man Par." How you fare in this contest determines the outcome.

The real opponent in this "conflict" however, is fought on another front, an internal one within oneself and the reactive stuff that has to be dealt with— the mental stresses: Self doubts, the upsetting memories, the self criticisms that continue to resurface and get in the way to the golfer's success.

---

73. necessity level: a sudden heightened willingness which untaps a tremendous amount of ability

Goals become thwarted and purposes fail; yet despite it all it's the golfer who hangs in there, persists, who continues to rise to the occasion and make things go right, despite all the reasons to give up or do something else—is the one who succeeds. Golf is a game of being patient and is one key attribute that great players of the game build their game around.

I can remember one of my first big golf matches, when I was ten years old and got upset in the match. I started crying over the fact that my opponent (my brother) didn't get on the green "in a pure way" while I had, yet he got it up and down, whereas I three-putted to lose the hole. My dad told me that there's no entry on the scorecard for form and how you get the job done—it's get the job done the best way that you can, make your game happen, and be the scoring threat that you are totally capable of being. The number of perfect rounds of golf that you have played or will play tells the tale.

It Takes Courage To Succeed

Golf is likely the most difficult of all sports to master. Golfers are a brave lot when it comes to tackling "Old Man Par." It takes courage to succeed despite the many invitations to fail. Each of us has a dream...a goal, a place in this game that we would like to achieve, be it winning the club championship, making the PGA Tour, winning a Major, or just being the best that we can.

Yet how many golfers have hung it up, lost the dream that flickers inside, and have decided to really just be a "spectator" of golf after all, and call the commentary at the nearby club, thinking of yesteryear, when they could throw a long iron in close, "feather" the pitch shot in close with some "stuff" on it...yet that flame only flickers now and then and is on the edge of extinction, living only through the identification with a promising young player, learning the ropes.

It Takes Courage to Win

It takes courage to stick to your dreams and make the best of your game. There doesn't seem to be enough of this attribute to go around amongst golfers. A word of caution! Don't let this scenario happen to you. NEVER GIVE UP YOUR DREAM. You are as alive as you have a dream.

Always set a new goal to achieve once you accomplish the current one. Acknowledge your triumphs, however small, and build upon your confidences. You'll need to persist through the rough times, there will be a number of these, just keep on charting your path, and going in the right direction, and you will arrive where you want to be. It's like moving up to the next rung of the ladder to further success. It's the small steps of hard won progress that denote success.

You need to continue to improve the present condition of your game to a better one. Things just do not remain the same with your golf. You're either putting well, hitting your irons good, but can't seem to hit your tee shot; there's always room for improvement.

The state or condition of your game is subject to flux on a continuous basis—so work on those areas that need the work from an analysis of your stats (greens hit in regulation, fairways hit, number of putts, etc). You have to have courage and perseverance to work at and play this game to win.

You've Got to Laugh a Little

Golf, being a mental game, can't be played seriously with an uptight, rigid attitude. Such an approach has no real long term value and will only end up in utter frustration, failure, and become too upsetting for the golfer to deal with. It was golf great, Walter Hagen, who said "that you got to stop and sniff the roses" on the way while you play.

It took over seven long years for the legendary Bobby Jones to win a major tournament, having been at the top of his game for that period before he broke through to win majors, and later golf's most coveted triumph, the Grand Slam. There aren't any real, bad tempered players, "John McEnroes" that make it on today's golf tour especially at the top. Patience is a real virtue in golf.

Being too serious or uptight accounts for more tourneys and matches being lost more than any other factor. Where the golfer's attention becomes too focused upon the penalty of losing, his intention turns to having to "win at all costs" and he begins to self destruct.

This self destruction marks the changing of the game with "Old Man Par" to the deadlier, more serious game of focusing more and more of the players energy on the outcome or consequence of his losing; the penalty of failure. For the golfer failing to perform is a harder opponent to deal with than "Old Man Par."

Good players who have put together successful winning performances play within themselves. They know that if they start invalidating their ability and allow their reactive minds to take over, they'll lose control of the situation.

They know that they must keep things in perspective, that golf is a game of barriers and obstacles, and its the player ability to meet these challenges that the game is all about.

Spirit of Play

This is something that you must keep in constant perspective in your golf, otherwise you will find that the game becomes no fun at all and is no longer a game, but a futile exercise in getting the best from you and bringing out the worst in you as well. In order to do your best and to win at golf you must have a spirit of play that is a reminder that golf is a game (to enjoy overcoming its challenges). It's not intended to be an internal war of getting the best of you unless you make it that.

You have to laugh and smile over those really horrible golf shots that you fire off in unknown directions, in order to take it all in stride. That's needed in this game to come out on top.

I can tell you that the only way that you will ever develop a Winning Approach and be a champion in your game has all to do with this "spirit of play" attitude. After many years of working with good players, I am convinced that this is the all-important ingredient—those who didn't have it didn't rise to the top—an attitude that's necessary for winning and it's a philosophy and discipline that you must live in order to do so.

I think that there are a number of great golfers from each generation that exemplify this attitude, who really loved the game. I think of players like Lee Trevino, Tom Watson, Jack Nicklaus, Walter Hagen, Bobby Jones, and Ben Hogan, who lived this philosophy: They loved golf.

The truly great players of the game do one thing time and again—they stick to what works in their game even down to the little things that have proven to work. They don't really fool around with their swings all that much, if at all unless there is a definite flaw that can be changed. They work

Winning attitude.

on perfecting their short game, their putting and wedge play around the greens. They know the importance of the scoring game.

These successful actions that have worked for the player are counted on again and again to work in their game and they become the cornerstone around which confidence is built. This is something that you as the golfer can cultivate in your game and will keep your game in tip top shape.

I hope you can use this information in this book to your advantage.

Here's to your golf game never being the same again. Wishing you success and the best in your golf!

Bob Cisco
The Ultimate Game of Golf

About the Book and the Author
The Author

This book, *The Ultimate Game of Golf* was fifteen years in the making! The idea for the book first came about back in 1975. It was in effort to handle my own game and failing ambitions to live up to what I considered was my life's dream: To play on the Pro Tour. I was determined to find a way to break the "impasse," to unburden what I felt was something that had been holding me back for years in my game—the mental aspects of the golf—and bring my game once again to the pinnacle that I knew I was capable of reaching.

Having been an excellent junior player, shooting in the 70s on a routine basis since I was twelve years old, and having broken eighty while ten years of age, my game started to decline and go downhill right about my sixteenth birthday. I was rather burned out, in a slump, and quite frustrated with what was occurring in my game. The day that I shot a lackluster seventy-five and was beaten by twelve shots by my brother, who forged a sixty three, I knew that something was wrong. "I had hit the wall" as they say.

I was struggling with my game, a bad attitude and temper that was second to none, while my brother was breaking the seventy barrier with some regularity. Neither I nor those around me or associated with my game knew what was really wrong. Yet it had all to do with the mental approach, this area wasn't part of the golf lesson that instructors taught, about which little was really known. This was before *Golf in the Kingdom* and *The Inner Game of Golf* had made their impact onto the scene in the '70s.

My frustration led to more disappointment and upset, and under such conditions, a player's concentration fails him. Negative thoughts crept more and more into my game, and my performance as I entered the ranks of collegiate golf was not "up to par." There was an Achilles heel that was not mending.

Collegiate golf was the place to perfect one's game and prove oneself as a promising player. It was a proving ground of competition that paved the way for the aspiring player to the pro ranks, if one's game were good enough.

For me however, my game didn't materialize fully and I didn't achieve the dream that I had sought and worked so hard for... I was disappointed to say the least. Golf didn't seem to be fun anymore, but seemed instead a deadly serious do or die activity.

My dream would have to for now take a back seat until I could find the answers somehow. A serious back injury made matters worse in 1978 in any real attempt at a comeback to play the Tour....

This book, *The Ultimate Game of Golf* represents that journey to find the answers to what had held back such a promising "rookie." When I broke eighty as a ten year old there was some talk around the club about "this kid being the next Arnold Palmer," and so forth.

The Ultimate Game of Golf is that path traveled not just by myself, but for all golfers who feel that they haven't reached their true potential. Deep down they know they could play far better golf if they could cast aside the negative doubts, fears, and lack of self confidence and find a way to bring their game to the higher level that they know they are truly capable of achieving.

There is a better way to play golf and play far closer to your potential than ever before. It achieves a higher state of mind and focus, and gives you a power of simplicity with the golf swing. With this approach, you achieve a sense of power and control like never before, that will bring about the "The Ultimate Game of Golf" Golfer in you.

I have over the last number of years been researching this area—studying, observing, and working with golfers of all levels, top pros, amateurs, and so forth, to compile a workable set of principles based on the natural laws of movement and those of human mental performance for the golfer.

It is my life ambition and career to help others play their best. Besides the improvemnt that players have gotten from the program (see the sample list of player profiles), I'm happy to report that I'm playing the best golf that I can using the principles and drills from this book. I'm back on track, hungry for the win and entertain the idea of a comeback myself.

*[The author won the Celebrity Centre International Golf Association's Tournament Player's Series in 1991! This award goes to the player who accummulates the highest total of points for the year. Bob won three tournaments in 1991.]

About The Book

The book really got going in the Fall of 1988 and it was at this point that I got busy and started getting down all the notes, observations and the advises that I had accumulated over the last several years from working with good amateurs and pros on Tour.

I formed *The Sports Advisory* in 1987, a consultancy to assist athletes who wanted to improve their mental performance and be the best they could at their sport, especially golfers, who know the importance of the mental game.

To date *The Sports Advisory* has produced over twenty five victories and over sixty-five top ten finishes amongst its players and there are more in its future plans. Perhaps it will be you!

Feel free to write me if you have a particular question about your game, care of *The Ultimate Game of Golf* at the address below.

Bob Cisco
C/O Griffin Publishing
544 W. Colorado Blvd.
Glendale, CA 91204

Player Profile Successes
on "The Ultimate Game of Golf" Program

Each player's performance was evaluated from which a tailored made program was worked up to strengthen the weak points and maintain the strong ones; thus working both ends into a series of doable steps that sharpened skills and ability.

These profiles highlight key points from "The Ultimate Game of Golf" Program that helped to improve the overall game of these players. They are set up in such a way that you can see the Before/After—where the player was before the program and how he improved afterwards and some of the recommendations taken.

PLAYER PROFILE # 1

Steve Huelsman. Age 43. Amateur from Los Angeles, California. Started playing golf at age 38. Goal: To be a scratch golfer.

Observation: When I first started working with Steve on his game, he was pretty wild off the tee, inconsistent with his iron play and overall shot-making skills. He was very long off the tee, 275-300 yards—when he hit it, but he didn't have the consistency to predict which fairway his drives would land in.

His alignment and set-up to the ball was a problem due to his height of 6'3". He used clubs that were two inches longer in length than normal, and he had difficulty in his address position, standing too close to the ball. This caused him to flex his knees and legs too much. The result was a restricted back swing move, which made his swing too up and down and wristy. He would lay the club over at the top of his backswing, which put the club off.* He did not have a pre-shot routine established at that time.

There also was the movement of the head going back with the takeaway in the backswing, which sped up the swing tempo, the cocking of the wrists

---

*off plane: out of postion. The angle of the club face is not in correct position to the ball and its center of rotation in the swing

prematurely which essentially created a disconnection of the arm swing from the rotation of the trunk or body.

He did have a good strength from which to build upon in his game: His putting and chipping which offset an inconsistent tee-to-green game.

The first major improvement that led to increased consistency in Steve's game was getting him properly aligned to the ball, which put him in a stronger position and more on plane with the target line. A video camera helped Steve to see what his swing was doing and where it was breaking down in performance.

The second area of improvement came several months later and was a combination of improved understanding of the mechanics of the swing, and of the mental approach in his game; notably from developing a consistent pre-shot routine that resulted in smarter thinking, and using a strategy for a better score.

Results: Steve dropped his handicap from 24 to 8 over a two year period on "The Ultimate Game of Golf" Program. Now breaks 80 on a regular basis. Shot personal best of 74. A much better golfer.

PLAYER PROFILE # 2

Terry Fine. Age 44 from Atlanta, Georgia. Had been playing golf on and off for over twenty-five years. An honorable mention collegiate All-American golfer in 1973. Goal: To play on the Senior Tour at age 50.

Observation: Terry had achieved some financial goals in life and always had the dream of playing competitive golf again. When the idea of a senior tour came up several years ago, it got him interested in making a comeback in his game. He would have five years to devote to practicing and getting ready for it. So he started working on his game. Terry started entering amateur competitions on the Golden State Tour while living in Los Angeles, California. He played in 10–12 of these events but did not break 80 in any of these although he was hitting a good number of greens and hit the ball relatively well.

I met Terry at one of these events and we later did an interview on his game to see what could turn things around.

The main area that came up was the inability to score under pressure and turn a potential good round into a good performance. He wasn't hitting the ball badly but there would be that one (or more) really bad drive that would get him into trouble. Also, he wasn't getting the ball up and down around the greens for par and was not hitting the wedge shot close from fifty yards and in on the par fives.

I tailored a program for him initially to 1) improve his consistency off the tee, 2) work on a series of practical drills on his short game which is vital for scoring, and 3) improving the mental approach. I worked out a pre-shot routine for Terry that he would use in practice and especially on the course for competition. We kept in a tight schedule, meeting several times a week, and worked on his game. After about four to five weeks of work on this, it was time to test it out in competition.

There was one rather significant problem that needed to be addressed and that was the decision to continue playing as an amateur versus a pro. I felt, based on Terry's input in wanting to have a bigger challenge that it was necessary for him to now turn pro. Coincidental with this decision was the fact that the Golden State Tour had changed its age requirement from fifty to forty-five years. The timing was just right to go for it.

It was a one-day tournament over in Pasadena, close to where I lived, so we decided to have me go to this event and "be in his corner": I would go the full eighteen holes with him. One thing that I had done for Terry's driving was to get him to extend the backswing further; this was getting him thirty additional yards off the tee which made a real difference as he was out-hitting his opponents consistently in his group.

After twelve holes he had gotten back to par and had a one-stroke lead. He birdied the thirteenth and had an outright chance of victory but the "old comfort zone" has a way to sneak up on one: Terry was in trouble off the tee on the sixteenth, where he almost hit his tee shot out of bounds. He was in trouble again at seventeen, the par three, where he again hooked his approach shot left into a sand trap close to the out of bounds. He finished at the eighteenth with a great drive down the middle and two putts from twenty-five feet for par four and the runner-up spot.

He realized that he had almost won his pro debut event, finishing second and for someone who had never won or finished higher than third in previous events, Terry felt elated beyond words...he became more confident about his game especially his driving and short game, where he applied the putting drills successfully. His putting had become superb right around twenty-seven putts on the average per round.

Results: Went from seven to one handicap on "The Ultimate Game of Golf" Program Finished second in his first Pro Senior event on The Golden State Tour and went on to win two of his next five starts on that Tour within a month and one-half period in 1989. An overall better player, who was playing excellent golf.

PLAYER PROFILE # 3

Cindy Scholefield. Age 24 yrs. from Malibu, California. An honorable mentioned All-American from UCLA. Curtis Cup selection in 1987. Won the Broadmoor Invitational, the first USGA Women's Mid-Amateur title and the California State Amateur that year after doing "The Ultimate Game of Golf" Program in late 1986. Goal: To turn pro and play on the LPGA Tour.

Observation: Cindy was a front runner in her matches, would build up a good lead, then would see that lead dwindle as her opponent came on strong, grabbed the lead and beat her at the end of the match. This was her pattern in competition. She had finished four times straight as quarter-finalist in the California State Amateur and couldn't breakthrough and win the big one for some reason.

Her ball-striking ability was very good. She had an excellent short game, and a solid overall game that was one of the best as an amateur in the state and in the country. Yet there was something in her mental approach in her performances that got in the way under pressure. So that was what needed to be changed in order to be the best that she could be and move on to the pro ranks.

I think that the key for Cindy in doing the program was knowing that there were areas in her game that were right. Plus the increased knowledge of how the mind worked; these acted as reinforcements and boosted her confidence.

Results: Her tee-to-green game was solid, supported by a great short game, especially the putting. "The How to Play the Game to Win" section helped her stay more in control and allowed her to win her first major amateur tourney, The Doherty Cup in Florida. The confidence that she could win led to her best competitive results in amateur golf. Turned pro in September 1988. Qualified for the LPGA Tour in 1990 and played her first season year on the LPGA in 1991. Finished 6th place at the Boston Classic that year.

Dr. Jeffry H. Blanchard. Age 38 from Del Mar, California, a chiropractor. Started playing golf in October of 1987 and broke eighty in February of 1989. Entered competitive tournaments on the Golden State Tour that year as an amateur; best finish twenty-fifth. Goal: To break into the pro ranks and play on the Tour. I started working with Jeff on both the mental and physical aspects of the game in the fall of 1989. After two and one-half months, he had two second place finishes and in February 1990, went on to win his first tournament!

Observation: Despite playing in the 70's on a regular basis, Jeff's game still lacked the necessary consistency to score well enough on a competitive basis. He had trouble off the tee hitting the driver in the fairway, hit on the average eight greens, putted fairly well, but did not have an impressive short game that would get the ball up and down where needed.

His game lacked the offensive punch and necessary scoring edge with the finesse shots, the wedge and lob shots from 50 yards and in putting. Jeff had a good mental attitude, didn't get upset, and basically kept in control due to his even disposition and keen interest to play the best that he could.

Before we could get to the mental approach, it was my assessment that Jeff needed to get a better grasp of the fundamentals of his swing, as he needed to have some areas reshaped and worked. I also found that his clubs weren't right for him and that he needed to be better club-fitted due to his tall height. The video analysis of his swing revealed that he was laying the club over into too flat a swing plane position at the top and that his hands were not hinging together as they should at this point in the backswing. This was one of the chief causes that he would hit some wild, inconsistent golf shots during a golf tournament.

Jeff's alignment to the ball was improved and we set a better angle of the spine for him to work the swing back and through on plane. This resulted in him controlling his power better and he became more offensive in hitting his drives more consistently with the driver and three wood off the tee.

Along with this approach, a great amount of attention was devoted to the short game, since this is where the pros excel. Jeff recognized this as the key to scoring in his game. This showed up in his scorecards, and in the statistics that he had kept—the number of greens missed and the percentage of "up and downs" he had, and where he needed to improve in the scoring

272

department in order to play well.

Since chipping (13%) and putting (43%) made up over 55–60% of the scoring strokes, I had Jeff devote more work on this area than ever before. Along with the putting drills that he would use, he needed to practice more forty to sixty yard wedge shots to get his wedge shots closer on the par fives, and get more birdies.

Results: This program resulted in an improved sense of feel around the greens and in better scores; his scoring average dropped from 77.5 to 74.5 in a period of four weeks. The combined improvement from the swing and the short game resulted in Jeff finishing second twice and winning his first tourney all within a three-week period on the Golden State Golf Tour.

PLAYER'S PROFILE # 5

Jeff Anderson. Age 25 from Poway, California. Golden State Tour Player. Best finish on the Golden State Tour was a fifth place finish. He came in to work on the mental side of the game after missing the PGA Tour School Qualifier in Fall of 1988.

Observation: Jeff's game was streaky, subject to a swing of up and down performances. He could shoot some very good scores under par, or would be in the high seventies.

Jeff was long off the tee, good with his irons, and a good putter on the whole. Where he needed improvement was in his wedge and sand play, and with his mental attitude in the game as he tended to get really down on himself when he performed poorly. The first approach that was taken was to improve the short game, the finesse shots around the green with the wedge. When he didn't get home in two on the par fives, he was not getting the ball in close enough with his wedge shot, to make easier birdies from under ten feet. He learned to hit the wedge better from forty yards and improved his sandshot from out of the trap as well.

In addition to his wedge play, I introduced Jeff to the putting drills/remedies that are now part of the Program. This produced a better sense of feel and sharpened his timing of the putting stroke. He had an improved stroke that he was more confident with. Since Jeff was playing in a lot of one-day events on the Golden State Tour, it was crucial to get off to a good start especially on the opening holes. We decided to have me come along and be his personal coach and in his corner throughout the round.

Results: This was an effective strategy as over the first opening holes we made a few changes on club selection and course management that paid off as Jeff was one under after five holes and in position to now "open up" and create more birdie opportunities, which he did, getting hot with the putter on the back nine, going on to birdie the last hole for 69, which won the tourney on a good course and a good field of players. All factors that we were working on in the Program came together over the next several weeks as Jeff won two events, finished third and fifth in the others and was playing great golf. Jeff Anderson went on to win more tournaments including the 1992 Sierra Nevada and Southern California Opens.

PLAYER'S PROFILE # 6

Bob E. Smith. Age 47 yrs. From Carmichael, California. Bob was a regular player on the Men's PGA Tour for many years and before that was a top ranked amateur champion in the U.S. In the past several years he had played on the European Tour and had one top ten finish there.

Observation: Bob's game has always been solid and showed his only weakness in shooting consistent sub-par performances. He could shoot under par but not often enough did he post scores under 68 or better when he needed to. Our analysis led to the area of the short game, especially the putting and his putting average confirmed this. Over the course of a four day tourney, this could amount to four to eight strokes due to this, despite hitting a lot of greens and having opportunities to score. The main thing that we did was to address the putting using some of the key drills/remedies from Section II of the Inner Game/Mental Approach on putting. These drills resulted in an improved awareness, an ability to concentrate better and a mental outlook towards putting as an opportunity to score. This worked extremely well and there was a positive change in Bob's putting with lower putts per tournament as a result.

Results: In the summer of 1989, he had four top ten finishes; his best at the English and Irish Opens, where he finished fourth. This was after he had had several sessions on "The Ultimate Game of Golf" Program, while in Los Angeles in May.

PLAYER'S PROFILE # 7

Bill Bowen. Age 43. Bill is an owner and president of a Title Reconveyance Tracking Co. His business is very demanding and doesn't give him the necessary time to work at his game. Goal: To shoot respectable golf, consistently in the 80s.

Observation: Bill tended to pick the club up going back in his backswing and would then cast or hit the ball from the top of the swing, thus hitting the ball with his upper body strength, instead of using his legs and lower body. This would produce an over the top, outside-in swing action, which would slice the ball off to the right. In order to compensate for this, Bill would play the slice, aiming farther to the left of the target, especially on his drives and irons, and just let the ball work back into the fairway or to the target.

His short irons were his strength, as he didn't slice the ball as much as he did with the longer shots. As a matter of fact, he hit these shots straighter or would pull them to the left. Bill's putting was pretty good for the most part. He had a pretty good touch in this department for the amount of time he had to practice and play.

Bill wasn't playing much golf and was concentrating more on work. He had in actual fact given up the game as he just wasn't getting any better.

The main areas that we worked on were his posture, how he was setting up to the ball, stabilizing the backswing, and his takeaway from the ball. Bill was getting disconnected in the swing: The larger muscles of the upper body weren't getting involved in the backswing, and as a result of this the hands were cocking too quickly and causing him to pick the club up.

I got Bill to concentrate on sweeping the club along the ground, which delayed the cocking of the wrists until about waist-high position. This helped him move more from his center and in doing so kept the triangle position between the arms and shoulders connected.

This got the torso and the rotation of the arm swing more synchronized. This resulted in a more powerful drive of the lower body (the hips, thighs, and legs) into the ball in the forward swing and out to the target. In addition to this, we worked on improving his chipping, sandshot, and long putts, using several of the putting drills from the book.

Results: Bill's scores moved down from the high 90s to the upper 80s, low 90s range all in a matter of eight weeks after the start of the program. He won low net (gross score—handicap) and had two second place finishes in his golf association's monthly tournaments.

PLAYER'S PROFILE # 8

Gary Beeny. Age 43. From Glendale, California. President of a Title Insurance Company in the Los Angeles area. Goal: To shoot more consistent golf and break 80.

Observation. Gary had a better swing than what his handicap showed, a 27 at the time, yet his problem in his game was more mental than anything else. His tee-to-green game was more like a 10–12 handicap golfer, but his downfall was the short game, and was killing his chances to score. He lost the majority of his strokes around the green. His wedge play and chipping were poor. His putting was fair. The key to turning his game around would have to come from improvement in the short game.

The main area that we worked on in his game was the scoring game. Our premise was that if he improved his pitching wedge shot, and his ability to get up and down in his chipping, that his confidence would soar and his scores would lower by 5–10 strokes.

In addition to this, we worked on improving his driving off the tee, as this area tended to be inconsistent and produced some tee shots that penalized his second shot. Gary's set-up position was changed, squaring up the shoulders, hips, and feet to the target. His takeaway was improved with the upper body (left shoulder and arms) leading back instead of the hands initiating the move back.

Gary was more consistent off the tee when he drove with his four wood; he was unusually long with this wood, hitting it as far as most golfers hit their driver.

Results: Gary's game, after a series of sessions, began to "fire on all cylinders", as his scores improved and he registered a personal best of 82 at Lakeside Golf Club, a difficult course in the Los Angeles area. His handicap dropped to 22 during the time he did the program.

PLAYER'S PROFILE #9

Taylor Lundries. Age. 19 yrs. From La Canada, CA.
Goal: To play competitive golf as a professional golfer or as a good amateur.

Observation: Taylor wanted to make the college golf team and continue to take his game to its highest level. His index at the time was 15.8 and he still lacked the consistency he needed to be considered for the golf team which was still a year away. He had recently been to a golf school in the S. California area and still was looking for the improvement when he came to me.

After doing an introductory session with Taylor, I took some notes on his game and found the following to be the case: His drives off the tee were long but lacked accuracy and at times were high to the right. Iron play was better but he tended to overswing and come over the top, losing his balance in doing so. Short game especially putting was his strength, averaging around 30 putts a round.

We worked on his fundamentals first and got his posture and alignment to the target more squared up with his shoulders, hips and feet. Since his shoulders were drooped some, we had him stand taller with his shoulders back more. This helped to eliminate tension in the shoulders and upper back region and helped set the plane better in his backswing.

By pushing the club more back in the backswing, instead of hinging his wrists earlier, he got better extension and consistency going with his swing. We also improved his short game especially with the wedge and after 12 weeks of working together, Taylor was in single digits for the first time, his index came down to a 8.9 and he had shot his best score ever, a 76 on his home course, Annandale C.C., a good course in the Los Angeles area.

PLAYER'S PROFILE # 10

Kevin Leach. Age 21. From Palos Verdes, California. Goal: To play on the Tour as a professional golfer.

Observation: Kevin was a standout junior golfer who went on to play for the UCLA college team. We met in the summer of 1986. He was long off the tee and a strong iron player and he could shoot impressive scores, but he tended to be streaky as a player. He needed to come up with the crucial shot more often to steady his performance and scores. He felt he became too serious at times during a tournament and he needed to improve his mental game.

The mental approach was the chief area of his game that was addressed. Concentration, a better pre-shot mental routine and attitude were the key factors from our discussions that needed work.

From our sessions on the mental game, Kevin realized that when the pressure was on and he had hit a bad shot or didn't make a needed putt, his concentration would disperse rather than become more focused. He would become too concerned and serious about what was wrong rather than accept a bad shot and move on to the next one. In doing so, Kevin abandoned his pre-shot mental routine and focused his attention on negative thoughts instead of the positive thought of planning the next shot.

Kevin found that seriousness did not lead to any successful resolution of his game and actually was harmful. It was important to keep in perspective that golf was a game and you had to enjoy it to excel at it.

Results: Improving his pre-shot mental routine led to a higher level of concentration and stability in his game and Kevin went on to have his best year in collegiate golf at UCLA, helping his team win the NCAA championships in 1989.

After sharpening his game further on the Golden State and various other Tours, Kevin qualified for the Ben Hogan Tour in 1991!

Contents

278

Glossary of Terms

*[NOTE: In this Glossary, technical terms have been defined to provide better understanding and clarity of the text. A number of the definitions, tagged with an asterisk, are quotes from the works of L. Ron Hubbard.]

Acknowledgement*: "'Something said or done to inform another that his statement or action has been noted, understood and received."

Adverse: Unfavorable, harmful.

Alignment: Arrangement or position in a straight line. In golf this is lining up or positioning the club and the body to the target, preferably in a straight line.

"All in the State of Mind": A popular poem having to do with the proper mental approach needed in golf and life, written by an unknown author.

Analytical*: "Capable of resolving problems, situations. The word analytical is from the Greek 'analysis' meaning resolve, undo, loosen, which is to say take something to pieces to see what it is made of."

Arc: The curved, elliptical path of the clubhead in the golf swing, in its motion back and through the ball.

Ariel, Dr. Gideon: Sports scientist and author of the book, *The Biomechanics of Power Golf.*

Assessment: An evaluation or appraisal. [Definition from Latin 'assidere,' "to sit beside"].

Athletic position: The ideal position in the golf swing in which the body is positioned, and which is maintained throughout the swing with emphasis on balance, posture, and alignment.

Attention*: "When interest becomes fixed, we have attention."

Attitude: A way of thinking, acting, or feeling. A feeling tied to how one views a particular subject or activity.

Axis point: The reference point around which the golf swing revolves.

Backswing: The swinging of the club back, up, and around the body. A preparatory move in which the body and club are loaded in a coiled position storing potential energy.

Balance: Steadiness, equality of weight, amount. In golf one of the main components of movement.

Balance point: The center of gravity around which motion of the golf swing occurs. A specific point in the body in which balance is maintained: the balls of the feet, second sacral segment of the lower back, the sternum, eyes, and ears are such balance points in the body.

Ballard, Jim: A professional golf instructor who has worked with a number of Tour players, most noticeably Curtis Strange. Author of the book, *How to Perfect Your Golf Swing/Using Connection and the Seven Common Denominators.*

Ballesteros, Séve: One of the best foreign players in modern golf, who won the Masters and The British Open in the 1980s. Known for his aggressive and daring play.

"Being in the Zone": A state of mind in which the golfer is totally focused, confident and relaxed and is playing effortless, rewarding golf.

Being Decisive in Strategy Drill: A drill that improves the role of decisiveness in strategy on the course.

Biomechanics: In golf, the study of the interactions of the body, its stress points, and the rotation of the golf swing through space and accelerated force in hitting a ball. [Derived from 'bios,' body + mechanics, the analysis of the action of forces on matter].

Bolt, Tommy: A golfer who played the PGA Tour in the 1950s–1970s, winning a number of tournaments including the US Open.

Boomer, Percy: Noted golf instructor and author of the book, *On Learning To Play Better Golf.* Boomer helped shape the fundamentals of modern day golf instruction.

Cause: To make happen; make do; bring about. Causative: Effective.

Centering: A principle in which movement is controlled, balanced, and coordinated. Its origin has to do with the martial arts and in Eastern philosophy.

Center of gravity: The balance point of the body (just below the navel) from which the golf swing is maintained, and controlled.

Centrifugal force: Mechanical—The resistance of the inertia in an orbiting object to change in direction. In golf—The tendency of the swinging clubhead to pull out away from the body in the forward swing, as the rotation of the left arm and body directs the motion into a straight line at the ball.

Chain reaction: A series of events, each of which influences its successor.

Choice: Power or chance to choose.

"Choking": An expression in golf in which a golfer is adversely affected by the pressure of a situation, and blows his chances.

Circuit*: "A division of your own mind that seems to make up another personality and this other personality affects you, argues with you and so forth."

Circuit Breaker Drill: A drill designed to break down tension in putting by making a fluid, rhythmic stroke and breaking down the negative circuit that has the player tied up in mechanics.

Close Encounter of the Golf Kind: An experience in golf that's out of the ordinary, in which the player experiences a heightened sense of confidence, feel, and power and plays above his potential.

Come over: An expression used in golf that denotes that the golfer's upper body, namely his right shoulder, has fired prematurely, and has crossed over in the forward swing to the target.

Common denominator: That factor that is present in each component.

Competent: Able, possesses demonstrated ability.

Comfort Zone: A coined expression that refers in golf to playing above your current level of ability or handicap.

Concentrate: Pay close attention to; direct one's attention to.

Concentration: The state or condition of being focused; directed attention. Doing what you are doing while you are doing it.

Confidence: Being able to predict, control the outcome of an activity. A feeling of competence.

Connected up: A term used in golf instruction that signifies that the torso, arms, and body rotation are working together as a powerful unit from the golfer's center of gravity.

Connection: The linking of the component parts of the golf swing in a synchronized manner. [Definition from the Latin 'conectere,' com, together, + 'nectere,' to bind.].

Consummate: To complete; fulfill; perfect.

Control: To command; rule. In golf to be able to initiate the swing, continue it, and bring the swing to its completion in a commanding way.

Corollary: A deduction or inference. A natural consequence or effect; a result.

Course Management: The state or condition of managing, being in control of one's mental and strategy game on the course during play. Checking for yardages and exact distances of pin placements on the green, and what clubs to use are such examples.

Cycle of Action*: "The sequence that an action goes through, wherein the action is started, is continued for as long as is required and then is completed as planned."

Decide: Settle; resolve; make up one's mind.

Decision: The act of reaching a conclusion or making up one's mind. Firmness of action; determination. [Derived from Latin 'decidere,' decide].

Decisive: Conclusive; characterized by decision and firmness.

Decisiveness: The act, state, or condition of being decisive, sure, and the acting upon that determination in a positive way.

Decisive/Indecisive Scale: A scale developed by the author that shows how decisive or indecisive a golfer is, and in what area of the game.

Dianetics*: "A science of the mind. Man's most advanced school of thought. An organized body of data. A popular self-improvement book written by L. Ron Hubbard."

Dimension: A measure of spatial extent, especially width, height, or length. The size or extent. [Definition from Latin, 'dimensio', a measuring, and 'dimensus,' to measure carefully].

281

Directing Your Attention Drill: A drill designed to improve the golfer's concentration and mental approach in golf.

Dramatize*: "To repeat in action what has happened to one in experience.... It's a replay now of something that happened then. It's being replayed out of its time and period."

Draw: A slight hook in which the ball travels right to left.

Drill: A specific task or exercise designed to develop a skill or familiarity with a procedure. A training exercise.

Driving: The basic action involved in hitting a golf shot: The body and club thrusts up against the left side position at impact. The whole idea of what the golfer is doing in the golf swing.

Dynamics of Movement: The fundamentals involved in the movement of the body in sports that have to do with a club, racquet, or bat. Having to do with the interaction of energy or force and motion.

Effect: Result; what is caused. Bring about; make happen.

Ellipse: Oval having both ends alike. The golf swing is an ellipse.

Emphasis: Stress; importance.

End Result: The outcome in the form of a product, result or skill that one can now use.

Engram*: "A mental image picture which is a recording of a time of physical pain and unconsciousness. It must by definition have impact or injury as part of its content."

Enigma: Puzzle, something inexplicable.

Enturbulate*: "Cause to be turbulent or agitated and disturbed."

Execute: Carry out; do. Put into effect. [Derived from Latin 'ex(s)equ, ex(s)ecutus', execute, follow to the end.

Execution*: "The act of carrying out an intention."

Fade: A slight left to right curve of the golf shot to a target.

Failed Purpose*: Fail: Not succeed; be unable to do or become what is wanted, expected or attempted. Purpose: "The survival route chosen by an individual, a species, or a unit of matter or energy in the accomplishment of its goal."

Faldo, Nick: Modern Tour player from England who has won The Masters and the British Open several times.

Feathering: The art of hitting golf shots in which a degree of finesse is required in shot-making , such as hitting the shot easier with a half or three-quarter swing, knocking the ball down in the wind, cutting the ball up high, etc..

Feel: The sensitivity or sense of touch in the hands and fingers of the golfer's grip. The correct estimation of effort required on a given golf shot.

Flexors: Muscles that act to flex a joint. [Definition taken from Latin, 'flectere', to flex].

Floated: The sensation created in the backswing when the weight is shifted via the center of the body to the back leg position.

Floyd, Raymond: Winner of numerous Tour events, including that of several major golf tournaments. Noted for his aggressive and decisive play.

Flow: To proceed steadily and continuously. To appear smooth, harmonious, and graceful. In golf, the harmonious interaction of motion and position.

Focus: A center of interest or activity. To concentrate on; to fix one's attention on with interest. Verb. [Definition taken from Latin, fireplace, hearth (the center of the home)].

Formula: An established procedure or method based on the principle or rule that when it is followed produces a desired result.

Free-swinging: Making a practice swing back and forth without the ball, with emphasis on a smooth flowing motion.

Function: Purpose; use; how something performs.

Gallwey, Tim: Author of the book, *The Inner Game of Golf,* and *The Inner Game of Tennis.* Covers the mental aspects of the sport.

Game*: A sport or other competitive activity governed by specific rules. A contest of person against person, or team against team. "A game consist of goals, purposes, and obstacles in which the objective is the overcoming of barriers and the attainment of the prize."

Game Plan: A term used in sports in which an athlete has a definite plan of how to overcome the opposition, usually based on his strengths.

Getting up and down: One of golf's vital statistics in the scoring game department in which the player converts three strokes around the green to two, by getting the short game shot (chip, pitch or sand shot) close enough to make the putt.

Goal: The desired end result; objective.

Golf: A game played on a large obstacle course, having a series of nine or eighteen holes, the object being to propel a small ball with the use of a club into each hole with as few strokes as possible. [Derived from Middle English].

Golf in the Kingdom: A book written by Michael Murphy that is a metaphysical tale of a golf game at "The Old Course" in Scotland.

Golf Is My Game: The name of the popular instructional book written by golfing great, Bobby Jones in the 1930s.

Gradient*: "A gradual approach to something, taken step by step, level by level, each step or level being, of itself, easily surmountable—so that, finally, quite complicated and difficult activities can be achieved with relative ease."

Grand Slam of Golf: Golf's four majors tournaments: The Masters, U.S. Open, British Open and PGA Championships. The "Slam" has only been won once, by golfing immortal Bobby Jones, in 1930.

Gravity: Natural force that causes objects to move or tend to move toward each other, especially the force exerted by a celestial body such as the earth. That force in golf which exerts resistance to the swinging club in the backswing and accelerates the club in the downswing.

"Gravity Golf": A term coined by the author to describe the role of gravity, momentum, and centrifugal force in the golf swing.

Grip: The club end that the golfer holds, which is opposite the head. The part of the club which is the handle. To hold or grasp securely the end-part or handle of the club. [Definition from Middle English, 'gripa', grasp, and from Old English, 'gripa', handful].

Hagen, Walter: One of golf's all-time greats; legendary player who won numerous tournaments and majors in the 1920–1930s era. Noted for his flamboyant, aggressive style of play.

Handicap: In golf, a rating system of playing that allows golfers to compete with one another based on their ability and experience.

Handling Stress and Indecision in Strategy Drill: A drill designed to deal with indecision and tension that can affect strategy and how to remedy this.

Hats: A term that denotes what function, activity, or job one is doing.

Haultain, Arnold: Author of the book, *The Mystery of Golf*, written in 1908, which was one of the first books written on the mental aspects of golf.

Held Positions: The positions of the body that interact and oppose one another in the golf swing. The base along with the motion of the swinging clubhead that creates power in the golf swing.

Hitting from Your Strengths Drill: A strategy drill that emphasizes the importance of playing from your strengths.

Hinge: A jointed or flexible device permitting turning or pivot of a part, such as a door, lid, or flap, on a stationary frame. In golf, having to do with the rotational action of the hands and wrists swinging around a fixed point in a circular plane and the role of the left shoulder [also see lever assembly].

Hogan, Ben: A legendary master of the game of golf who won numerous golf tournaments and major titles during the 1940s–1960s era. Known for his great shot-making and ability to concentrate.

Hub: The center point of a wheel. In golf the point around which the golfer swings the club on an inclined plane.

Hubbard, L. Ron: American author and philosopher. Author of *Dianetics, The Modern Science of Mental Health,* other self-improvement books, and Scientology applied religious philosophy.

Indecisive: Being uncertain, doubtful. Not carrying through one's intention.

Indecisiveness: The state or condition of being uncertain (in one's shot making or mental approach in golf).

Inner Game: The mental game, psychological side, or mental approach to the game of golf.

Inner Game of Golf: A popular book on the mental game of golf, written by Tim Gallwey.

Intention*: "1. An intention is something that one wishes to do. He intends to do it; it's an impulse toward something. 2. Intention is the command factor as much as anything else. If you intend something to happen, it happens." [From Latin 'intendio,' stretching out from 'intendere,' to stretch toward].

Intention Drill: A drill designed by the author of the *Ultimate Game of Golf* book in which the use of intention is drilled in the mental approach to golf.

Interlocking Grip: One of three grips used in golf in which the index or forefinger of the left hand is interlocked with the last finger of the right hand.

Interplay of Held Positions: The dynamic principle of movement in sports especially in golf, discovered by the author.

Introversion*: "Looking in too closely."

Invalidation*: "Refuting or degrading or discrediting or denying something someone else considers to be fact."

Jones, Bobby: Legendary golfer, who won twelve major titles including the Grand Slam of Golf in 1930. Authored several excellent books on the subject, including instructional films considered to be classic. Founder of the Masters Golf Tournament.

Keeping the Ball in Play Drill: This is a strategy drill designed by the author to improve optimum positioning and shot-making during play.

Kelly, Homer: Author of the book, *The Golf Machine,* which describes the golf swing in geometric terms and concepts.

Keys: A predominant thought or sense of movement that the golfer places his attention on while executing the shot to the target.

Key-In*: "A moment when the environment around the awake but fatigued or distressed individual is itself similar to the dormant engram. At that moment the engram becomes active. It is keyed-in and can thereafter be dramatized."

Kinesthesia: The sensation of bodily position, presence, or movement through spatial dimensions. [From the Greek word 'kinema', motion].

Kinetic: Of, relating to, or produced by motion. [Derived from Greek, 'kinetikos', moving, from 'kinein', to move].

Kismet: Fate; fortune. [Derived from Turkish 'kismet'; from Arabic 'qismah', lot].

Kite, Tom: One of the best modern day players of golf and the all-time leading money-winner on the PGA Tour.

Knee Knocker Drill: A putting drill to improve concentration on the short three-to-five foot range putts.

Knock down: A golf shot in which the player hits down on the ball, holding his release through the ball causing the ball to fly lower under the wind with spin on the shot.

Lagging: The sensation and phenomena of the club following behind the lead of the hands and body as the golf club is swung back and through to the ball at impact.

Lag/Lagging up: On long putts, to get one's approach putt to end up close of the hole.

Lateral: To move in a sideways direction. In golf, the movement of the lower body back and through from a central point in the swing. [Definition taken from the Latin 'lateralis', side].

Law: A formulation of the observed recurrence, order, relationship, or interaction of natural phenomena: laws of motion.

Lay up: A strategy in which the golfer hits his approach shot short of the target or green in an an effort to capitalize on a better position to hit the next shot to the hole. Usually done where the risk involved, such as water hazards or out of bounds, would penalize the player in playing too aggressively to the hole in his shot-making.

Leadbetter, David: A popular golf instructor who has worked with a number of top players of the game, including Nick Faldo. Author of the book, *The Golf Swing*.

Lever: In golf, the interactive role of the left arm and club as it's swung back around and up, and the drive of the straightening right arm at the ball at impact.

Lever assembly: The action of the left arm in the golf swing as it is pulled back towards the ball in the downswing. This motion causes the generation and transference of kinetic energy at the ball and impact.

Linking up: An expression denoting the component parts of the swing and how they "hook up" or connect.

Locke, Bobby: A Hall of Fame golfer from South Africa, considered to be one of the finest putters ever. He played on the U.S. and International Tour from 1940 to 1960s.

Look at the Hole Drill: A drill that helps free up and improve rhythm and timing in the putting stroke.

Lose*: "Intending to do something and not doing it, and intending not to do something and doing it."

Masters Golf Tournament: One of the golf's four major tournaments played in Augusta, Georgia, in April of each year. Founded by Bobby Jones.

Mechanics: The analysis of the interaction of force and motion in the golf swing.

Mechanism: Any system of parts that operate or interact like those of a machine.

Medal: A competition in golf in which the contest is decided by the total stroke play of the contestants. The player with the lowest score for the round or tournament is the winner.

Mental: Of or pertaining to the mind; intellectual. Done or performed by the mind. Adjective. [Derived from Latin 'mentalis,' from 'mens,' mind].

Mental Approach: That which the player thinks, conceives, and intends to have happen, including his attitudes and considerations associated with it. This approach follows a definite order from conceptualization, to final outcome (execution) in the hitting golf shots to a target.

Mental Aspects: Those elements that comprise the mental side of the game of golf.

Mental Image Picture*: "Copies of the physical universe as it goes by."

Mental key: A chief thought that is used by the golfer on the mental game to execute the swing at its highest level of intention. Decisiveness is a good example of such a "key."

Mental "stuff": The accumulated difficulties, upsetting memories, loses, and upsets that the golfer has endured over the duration of playing golf.

Method: A means or manner of procedure; especially a regular and systematic way of accomplishing anything. [Definition from the Greek word, 'methodos', a going after, pursuit].

Mind*: "The purpose of the mind is to pose and resolve problems relating to survival and to direct the effort of the organism according to these solutions."

Mind's Eye Drill: A putting drill designed by the author that teaches the use of visualizing the stroke and knocking the putt into the hole or lagging a long putt close to the hole.

Mind Game: The game that's enacted in the player's mind, that directs all estimation of efforts, and intentions towards one final result; winning.

Momentum: The force with which a body moves, the product of its mass and its velocity. [Definition from Latin, 'momentuom', motion, movement]. In golf, the combined action of the accelerating pivot of the body and the motion of centrifugal force in the swing.

Motion: The action or process of change of position of the body in space. In golf, motion is the moving of the body and club in the swing. [Derived from Latin, 'motio', from 'movere', to move].

Movement: Change of location. In golf, movement refers to the motion of the swing and body, back and through to the target.

Murphy, Michael: Author of the book, *Golf In The Kingdom*, a metaphysical tale in which a golfer's game is revitalized by the inner truths of golf by a wizened Scottish "caddie."

Muscles: A tissue composed of fibers capable of contracting and relaxing to effect bodily movement.

Natural laws: A formulation of the observed recurrence, order, relationship, or interaction of natural phenomena.

Natural Laws of Movement: A principle of movement in sports that involve motion and the hitting of a ball with a club or similar object.

Necessity level*: "A sudden heightened willingness which untaps a tremendous amount of ability."

Nelson, Byron: A legend of golf who played on the Tour in the 1940s, who won numerous tournaments and set a record of lowest scoring average (68.25) and most consecutive victories (11) in 1945.

Nicklaus, Jack: A legend of golf who many consider the greatest player of the game, winner of 22 major titles in his career.

Norman, Greg: A popular player on the PGA Tour, noted for his aggressive play and long drives. Winner of a number of tournaments, including the British Open.

Observation: The act of looking; seeing as is without bias or prejudice.

Off plane: An instructional term referring to the angle of the club face in which the club is not in the correct position to that of the baseline (ball) and its center of rotation to the target.

"Old Man Par": The golf course itself and its barriers that comprise it. The expression coined to describe playing against the golf course and par.

On plane: A term used in golf instruction that denotes the hands and club face are in the correct position or angle in relationship to the ball (baseline) and its center of rotation.

Outer Game: That part of golf having to do with the swing and its mechanics. Pertaining to the swing, and its fundamentals.

Overlapping grip: The grip used by the majority of golfers (90%) today, made popular by golfing great, Harry Vardon. In this grip, the last finger of the right hand overlaps or fits between the first and second finger of the left hand.

PGA: The Professional Golfers Association. An association of golfers which fosters the playing of golf and conducts the business of staging tournaments, instruction, and the sale of golf related items.

Physics: The science of energy and matter and of interactions between the two. Having to do with physical properties, interaction, processes, or laws. [Derived from Latin translation 'physica', natural science].

Pivot: To turn around or rotate around a fixed center point.

Pivoting: Turning or rotating around the body in the golf swing.

Plane (line): A line on a flat surface to be considered its baseline and the line along which that plane is to be rotated when changing its angle. Golf: A line inscribed on the surface of the inclined plane passing through the ball location to serve as its base and its center of rotation when changing its angle. Ben Hogan, in his book used a "sheet of glass" to describe the plane and the necessary path in which the golfer swings the club.

Planting: The braced, connected, athletic position that the golfer aligns to the ball and target.

Player, Gary: One of modern day golf's greatest players, who has won over 132 tournaments world-wise, including a number of majors. From South Africa.

Postulated*: "1. To cause a thinkingness or consideration. Causative thinkingness. 2. A postulate infers conditions and actions rather than just plain thinks. It has a dynamic connotation. 3. [From the word Postulate: that thing which is a directed desire, or order, or inhibition, or enforcement, on the part of the individual in the form of an idea. 4. He posts something. He puts something up and that's what a postulate is]."

Pool Table Drill: A putting drill made up by the author to improve hand-eye coordination and timing in the stroke.

Power: The interaction of held positions and opposing motions in the golf swing in which clubhead speed is generated by hitting up against the left side. Maximum clubhead speed is the result of each of these components working together.

Power connection: The athletic position in which the golfer is planted or braced. This connected position allows the linking up of the upper and lower body components in the golf swing, and generates clubhead speed, in which momentum, pivoting, and drive are maximized.

Premise: A proposition upon which an argument is based or from which a conclusion is drawn. [Derived from Latin 'praemissus' and 'praemittere,' to send ahead].

Present time*: "The time which is now and which becomes the past almost as rapidly as it is observed."

Pre-putt Mental Routine Drill: A putting drill that works on the mental approach using a pre-putt routine to improve concentration and delivery of the stroke.

Pre-shot mental routine: A precise series of steps that the player uses in the contemplation and hitting of the golf shot. A routine that good players use in their games that improves concentration and decisiveness.

Pre-shot Mental Routine Drill: The drill that employs the Pre-shot Mental Routine and each of its steps in sequence.

Primary focal point: The target is the primary focal point in golf.

Professional*: "It isn't magic or luck that makes the professional. It's hard-won know how carefully applied. A true professional may do things pretty easily from all appearances, but he is actually taking care with each little bit that it is just right."

Psychology: The study of stimulus-response mechanisms and behavioral characteristics. [Altered definition derived from the Greek word 'psychos,' soul, 'ology,' study of].

Punch: A golf shot in which you hit down on the ball causing it to fly low towards your target.

Purpose: Plan; aim; intention; something one has in mind to get or do.

Putt with Your Eyes Closed Drill: A putting drill that helps improve the tempo of the stroke and concentration.

Putting: That part of golf in which the golfer is on the green and makes a light stroke in an effort to place the ball in the hole.

Reactive Mind*: "A portion of a person's mind which works on a totally stimulus-response basis, which is not under his volitional control, and which exerts force and the power of command over his awareness, purposes, thoughts, body and actions."

Rehearse: Practice, repeat, go over again until one has it; drill.

Restimulator*: "Restimulators are those approximations in the environment of an individual of the content of an engram."

Rekindle: Revitalize; rejuvenate, get going again.

Release: To unload the stored potential build up of the swing into the ball in the forward swing.

Reverse pivot: A pivot that the golfer makes in which the weight stays or ends up on the left side of the body, causing him to throw, or release the club more from the top of his swing, and come over the shot.

Rhythm: Any kind of movement characterized by the regular recurrence of strong and weak elements: The rhythm of the tides. [From Latin, 'rhythmus,' from Greek 'rhuthmos', recurring motion, measure, rhythm]. In golf, the repeating motion of the swing buildup and the unloading of the swing through the ball.

Rotary: Of, pertaining to, causing, or characteristic by rotation, especially axial rotation. A part or device that rotates around an axis. [From the Latin 'rota,' wheel].

Rotation: The motion of the body and arm swing around a fixed axis point (the spine) and back through to the ball in the golf swing.

Routine: A prescribed and detailed course of action to be followed regularly; a standard procedure. A set of customary and often mechanically performed procedures or activities. [Derived from Old French, from 'route' (beaten path)].

Scale: A series of steps or degrees. A progressive classification, as of size, amount, importance, or rank. The proportion used in determining the relationship of a representation to that which it represents. Noun. [Definition taken from Latin, 'scalae', stairs].

Scientology: *"1. The science of knowing how to know. 2. The study of the human spirit in its relationship to the physical universe and its living forms. 3. [Formed from the Latin word scio, which means know and the Greek word logos, which means THE WORD, or

OUTWARD FORM BY WHICH THE INWARD THOUGHT IS EXPRESSED AND MADE KNOWN]."

Second sacral segment: A triangular shaped bone made up of five fused vertebrae that is located at the posterior section of the pelvis. The balance point or center of gravity of the body.

Secondary focus: The ball is not the primary point of interest in hitting the ball, the target is. The ball is the secondary focal point.

Scoring/Strategy Game: That part of golf that has to do with the positioning or placement of one's shots (strategy) and getting the ball into the hole in the least amount of strokes (scoring).

Senior: Above others in rank or length of service. Having preference in making certain decisions. [Definition from Latin, 'senex', old]

Seriousness*: "When interest is important because of penalty."

Setting up the Hole/Shot Drill: A strategy drill designed to teach how to play a given golf hole based on one's strengths and ball striking.

Shanking: to strike the ball in the neck or hosel causing the ball to veer rapidly to the right.

Snead, Sam: One of the greatest golfers of all time, played the Tour from the late 1940s–1970s. Winner of 135 Tour events, which include the Masters, British Open, and PGA championships.

Software: The written programs that tell the computer what actions to do and perform.

Spine angle: How the golfer stands to the ball and distributes his weight determines the angle of the spine in the golf swing. The golfer ideally should stand with shoulders erect, and bend from the waist and hips, which lowers the arms to meet the ball.

Square to Square Method: A swing approach devised by Bryon Nelson, and made popular in a book that he authored on the technique.

Stance: The position of the feet of the golfer when making a stroke. [Definition taken from Old French 'estance', position, place].

Start-Change-Stop*: "The anatomy of control. The cycle of action is seen in the turning of a simple wheel. The wheel starts and then any given spot on it changes position and then the wheel is stopped."

State of Mind: The mental or psychological condition of the individual, his current emotional response to the various things around him in his environment. [Definition taken from Latin 'status', manner of standing, condition, position, attitude].

Static: Having no motion; at rest. [Definition taken from Latin 'statikus', from Greek 'statikos,' causing to stand, placed].

Sternum: The breastbone. [Definition taken from Latin, from Greek 'sternom,' breast, breastbone].

Sticking to Your Game Plan Drill: A drill on the strategy game in which the player is taught to play from his strengths and to stick to that which produces results in course management.

Stimulus-response: Stimulus: Anything causing or regarded as causing a response. Something that incites to action. A reaction to a specific stimulus.

Stops: Obstacles and barriers that get in the way to one's performance in golf and in life.

Strength(s): The strong points in the golfer's game from which a game plan can be formulated.

Strategy: A plan of action to follow or execute in planning the hitting of golf shots to a target.

Strategy Game: The scoring game in golf that requires knowledge and smart thinking of where, how, and when to hit shots to the target.

Strategy Key: Having to do with the planning and execution of the golf shot. That predominate thought, or "key" that the player employs in regards to the placement of his shots on a given hole or course.

Stressful: Anything that has a point of difficulty, strain, or tension associated with it that sticks one's attention to it.

Stroke: A back and through striking action of the ball, especially that performed by the putter or chipper. A single completed movement or recorded motion in one's golf score.

Survey: To gather all applicable data and information so that one can decide upon a course of action. In golf the first step of the pre-shot mental routine as outlined by the author.

Swing: To move back and through in a rhythmic motion; to turn in place, as on a hinge or other pivot; the action of moving the club and body back and through in a smooth motion.

Swing key: A predominant thought or essential idea that the golfer "keys" on or uses to make the swing motion.

Synergy: Working together in combination or unison.

Tai Chi Chaun: A form of martial arts that is used as a calistenic for health in both the Orient and Western world. Noted for its mental discipline and powers of concentration.

Takeaway: The part of the golf swing which refers to the beginning of the backswing.

"Taking the gas": A term coined to mean that the golfer blew his chances, choked, or reacted to the pressure.

Target: The objective that one is trying to attain, goal. The object that the golfer is hitting the ball to.

Tempo: The velocity or speed at which something is moving or is being propelled. In golf this is the rate at which the club is being swung.